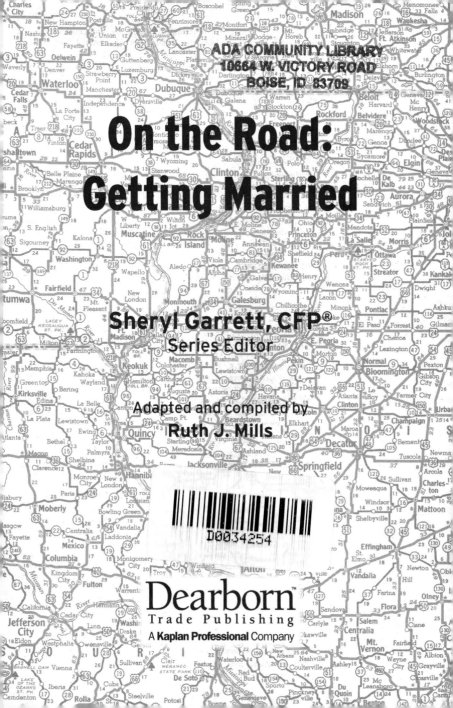

ADA COMMUNITY LIBRARY
10664 W. VICTORY ROAD
BOISE, ID 83709

On the Road: Getting Married

Sheryl Garrett, CFP®

Series Editor

Adapted and compiled by

Ruth J. Mills

Dearborn™
Trade Publishing
A Kaplan Professional Company

332.024
ON THE ROAD

This publication is designed to provide accurate and authoritative information in regard to the subject matter covered. It is sold with the understanding that the publisher is not engaged in rendering legal, accounting, or other professional service. If legal advice or other expert assistance is required, the services of a competent professional person should be sought.

President, Dearborn Publishing: Roy Lipner
Vice President and Publisher: Cynthia A. Zigmund
Senior Acquisitions Editor: Mary B. Good
Cover Design: Design Solutions

© 2006 by Dearborn Financial Publishing, Inc.

Published by Dearborn Trade Publishing
A Kaplan Professional Company

A Stonesong Press Book

Project Manager: Ellen Schneid Coleman
Interior Design: Brad Walrod/High Text Graphics, Inc.

All rights reserved. The text of this publication, or any part thereof, may not be reproduced in any manner whatsoever without written permission from the publisher.

Printed in the United States of America

06 07 08   10 9 8 7 6 5 4 3 2 1

Library of Congress Cataloging-in-Publication Data
Getting married/edited by Sheryl Garrett; adapted and compiled by Ruth J. Mills.
    p.   cm.—(On the road)
  Includes index.
  ISBN 1-4195-0047-3 (5 × 7.375 pbk.)
  1. Married people—Finance, Personal.   2. Finance, Personal.
I. Garrett, Sheryl. II. Mills, Ruth J. III. On the road (Chicago, Ill.)
HG179.G467 2005
332.024'01'08655—dc22   2005015089

Dearborn Trade books are available at special quantity discounts to use for sales promotions, employee premiums, or educational purposes. Please call our Special Sales Department to order or for more information at 800-621-9621, ext. 4444, e-mail trade@dearborn.com, or write to Dearborn Trade Publishing, 30 South Wacker Drive, Suite 2500, Chicago, IL 60606-7481.

Contents

And we've included "Postcards" that tell helpful stories of how other people have made successful financial journeys.

Finally, the end of the book includes an "Itinerary" or recap that reviews the key actions you should take at each major point in your life, all of which are discussed in detail in the seven chapters of this book. The end of the book also includes a list of other books to turn to if you want more indepth information on buying a home, saving for college, or getting insurance coverage.

We hope you find this "travel" guide helpful as you map your route to financial success and peace of mind. Life is an adventure, and money paves the way. So let's get started on the road: The light is green, put your pedal to the metal, and go!

Introduction

On the Road: Getting Married is part of a new series of books from Dearborn Trade Publishing intended to help you deal with the financial issues, problems, and decisions concerning specific life events. The decisions you face when you're getting married are often different from the decisions you'll make decades from now, when you're closer to retirement, for example. You're building a new life together, so you need to consider not only how your lives will merge, but also how your finances will!

Because financial planning shouldn't be intimidating, we've created these books to take away the terror. On the Road books are like travel guides to help you make the best financial decisions at each stage of your life, in this case as you get married and start your new lives together. This book addresses the issues that concern you *now* and will help you

- ▶ decide how you want to spend and save your money;
- ▶ make a budget you both can live with;
- ▶ get a mortgage and buy a home;
- ▶ make sure you have the right insurance (and enough of it) to protect you and your family;
- ▶ plan for retirement so you'll have enough money to live comfortably;
- ▶ make a will and do estate planning, to ensure your assets go where you want them to;
- ▶ save and make investments for your kids' college education, and handle taxes as a married couple.

These financial decisions are part of your life's journey, so we've made them easy to navigate, with lots of helpful "Roadmaps" (charts and tables of financial information to help you with each issue or decision that comes up), "Tollbooths" that help you calculate your expenses or savings, and "Hazard Signs" that caution you about some money pitfalls to watch out for. We've also included a section called "What to Pack," so you'll know the forms and other information you will need to get a mortgage, for example. We've made sure you'll know what we're talking about, by providing "Learn the Language" definitions of unfamiliar or technical terms particular to each financial topic.

Planning Your Trip Together

How to Budget, Save, and Spend Your Money

Getting married offers lots of financial benefits: You have two incomes that can help you pay your rent or mortgage and other bills, and you have twice the saving power to achieve your financial goals. Two can't live as cheaply as one, but your money should go a lot further.

Before you set off down this road, you should have a realistic idea of your current financial status. This chapter reviews the three most important things you need to do financially: how to discuss your finances and how you want to save or spend your money, how to create a budget that both of you can live with, and how to determine your short-, medium-, and long-term financial goals.

▶ Don't Go Down this Road! The Top 12 Money Mistakes People Make

For couples who are just starting their financial journey together, the best place to begin is to become aware of the top 12 money mistakes people make so you can avoid them.

▶ *Mistake #1. Not living within your means.* If your credit card bills are painful, you may know already that you're spending more than you should. Perhaps that's why you picked up this book. This is a good time to ask yourselves, "What are our long-term financial objectives?"

▶ *Mistake #2. Failure to set goals.* If you don't know where you're going, you may end up somewhere unpleasant. Whether you dream of long-term financial security, a Harvard education for your kids, the best of care for elderly parents, or retirement on a tropical island, you haven't taken control of your financial future if you haven't identified and prioritized your goals. Once these goals are established, you can make spending and investment decisions that will lead you in the right direction. (Setting goals is discussed in greater detail at the end of this chapter.)

▶ *Mistake #3. Not saving enough.* Figuring out how much you need to save can be complicated, but chances are you need more than you think. Because people are living longer, your retirement nest egg may need to last 25 to 35 years or more. You will probably also want to provide an income that will be adequate for your lifestyle and will keep up with inflation.

▶ *Mistake #4. Failure to create and stick to a budget.* Few people create a budget and stick to it. Yet people often find that once they've taken control of their finances by goal setting, planning, and budgeting, the resulting sense of well-being far outweighs any disappointment they feel from not spending as much.

▶ *Mistake #5. Too much debt.* Ideally, a home mortgage is all the debt one should have. It's considered "good debt" because your home appreciates or adds to its value over time and the mortgage interest is tax deductible. For most people, however, this plan is just not realistic. They need to borrow to buy automobiles and make other major purchases. Here are three guidelines to help determine your maximum level of debt.

1. Monthly housing expenses (your rent or mortgage payment, real estate taxes, and insurance) should be less than 28 percent of your combined pretax incomes.

2. Total monthly debt payments should be less than 36 percent of pretax income.

3. Consumer debt payments should be less than 20 percent of after-tax income.

Try to stay below these limits. Carrying credit card balances month to month (paying the minimum) is an absolute no-no. If you can't pay your monthly credit card bills in full each and every month, then you're living beyond your means—period.

▶ *Mistake #6. Failure to maintain an appropriate amount of cash reserves.* Most people should keep the equivalent of three to six months' worth of expenses in liquid accounts that they can access quickly for emergency funds. The lower amount may be adequate for two-career couples; the higher amount is better if your income is volatile or your family has only one wage earner. Unless special circumstances arise that require you to have more cash available, it's undesirable to keep excess cash in low or non-interest-bearing accounts because inflation eats away your money's purchasing power over time.

▶ *Mistake #7. Insufficient disability insurance coverage.* You are more likely to suffer loss of income due to a prolonged illness or injury than you are to die prematurely. In addition, the financial consequences of a disability to your family can be disastrous. Not only will your income stop, but expenses will rise due to the costs of treatment, rehabilitation, or long-term care.

▶ *Mistake #8. Failure to keep an up-to-date will.* If you die intestate (without a will), your state of residence will determine how your assets are distributed. Estate planning is critical if your assets are more than $1.5 million (including life insurance and the equity in your home). To avoid having your hard-earned assets eaten up by unnecessary taxes, you should explore strategies to minimize your taxes with a qualified attorney. Even if you don't have a lot of money, be aware that minor children become wards of the state if parents die without a will. In these cases, the state ultimately chooses their guardians. Don't put off until tomorrow what you could be doing today.

▶ *Mistake #9. Failure to diversify your savings and investments.* Simply stated, diversification means not putting all your eggs in one basket. Diversification also means spreading your assets among several different types of investments, such as stocks, bonds, cash, and real assets or commodities (oil, corn, cattle, and gold, for example). Diversification among different asset classes, or asset allocation, is beneficial because it can lead to higher returns and decreases risk over time.

▶ *Mistake #10. Too much focus on short-term investment results.* Your asset allocation and investing strategy should be based on your age, life circumstances, and the time when you expect you will need the assets.

▶ Mistake #11. *Failure to get advice from an expert when needed.* Most people never seek professional financial advice. Its cost is small when compared with the potential losses you may incur because you have chosen not to seek help. A growing number of fee-only financial planners will address your concerns by working with you on an hourly, as-needed basis without account minimums, long-term contracts, or commission-based bias. At a minimum, you should get professional help when you are trying to find the answers to the following questions:

1. How much will we need for retirement?
2. How much will we need for our children's education, and what are the best ways to fund it?
3. How much should we save on a regular basis to achieve our financial goals?
4. How can we best allocate our portfolio among different asset classes?
5. What are the best options when approaching a major life transition, such as a new job, marriage, home purchase, the birth of children, or retirement?

▶ *Mistake #12. Not being an educated investor.* Managing your money is a lifetime project, so continue to work diligently and become better informed. Reading this book and credible magazine and newspaper articles and listening to reliable experts are all great ways to get started. Be alert for hidden agendas and biases, and don't listen too closely to the daily news and stock market talk. Think long-term!

Educating clients is a major objective of a good financial planner, so if you opt to work with one, make sure they are willing and able to explain things clearly. In addition, both of you should be involved: Too many people rely on their spouses or partners to make all the household financial decisions, which causes them to be unprepared to handle the finances when the unthinkable happens.

▶ The Beginning of Your Journey: Where Do You Start?

Marriage brings many changes in a couple's financial situation that will affect goals and objectives, personal property, assets, debts, retirement accounts, savings, taxes, and more. However, with proper planning and good communication, two people can combine their assets and live nearly as cheaply as one with a better quality of life and standard of living than if they remain single. Here's a quick overview of the issues you should consider.

Handling Bank Accounts

One of the first challenges for a couple is how to manage their checking accounts. The most common options include combining all accounts right away or keeping three separate checking accounts: his, hers, and ours. Whatever the agreement, it is critical for each of you to have your own "fun" money to be used as each of you desires. If one of you wants to hit the golf course and the other wants to run by the manicurist, the "fun" money provides freedom and independence without guilt.

You might also want to make a list of all of your assets: his, hers, and jointly owned assets (if you've already bought a home, for example). Then list all your regular expenses: his, hers, and ours. Finally, list your incidental expenses. Because incidental items can add up quickly, you want to know where your cash on hand is going. This chapter will discuss incidentals in greater detail in the budgeting section when it discusses how you can watch out for "money magnets."

Talking about Finances

Small financial problems often grow into larger ones, simply because some couples find it difficult to talk about money. Financial problems are the number one reason that couples argue and are the leading cause of divorce. Before marriage, many people avoid the subject, in the belief that their partners are fiscally fit, only to find out that they are deeply in debt or have other problems managing money.

Before and during your marriage, it is important to communicate openly about money on a regular basis and keep each other informed of the financial situation. As your financial discussions progress, you will get a good sense of each other's spending habits and freely share your dreams for the future.

Many couples set aside time each week or each month for a financial discussion and reward themselves afterward with a dinner out or a movie.

Budgeting

Before you can make any financial decision, you need to know the value of what you own, how much you owe, how much you bring in monthly after taxes, and where your money goes each month. The next section of this chapter covers these aspects in detail, but here's a quick overview of what you need to do.

1. Collect all your financial documents (bank and credit card statements, checkbooks, information on assets and debts, employer benefit packages, and so on).
2. Put together a combined balance sheet listing all of your assets and debts. Set aside money for an emergency fund with living expenses for three to six months.
3. Determine what you are spending your money on and try to spot areas where spending can be reduced.
4. Review your combined investment portfolios. Rebalance them if your combined portfolios are overweighted in any particular asset class.
5. Find ways to maximize contributions to your retirement funds.
6. Obtain a copy of your credit report to see if any issues will affect your future borrowing power.
7. Split up financial duties between the two of you, such as paying the bills, consolidating statements, and keeping tabs on your savings. Then assign responsibilities based on each person's strengths. Or you can assign duties to the spouse who needs to develop a particular skill, and then have the other spouse provide coaching. Regardless of how you split, be sure to get together frequently to inform each other.

Changing Beneficiaries and Creating or Modifying Wills

When you get married, you will want to change the beneficiaries on your accounts, including your 401(k)s, IRAs, and life insurance. You will also need a will so that your assets are disbursed (distributed) properly when you die. If either of you have children from a previous marriage, a will is especially important to ensure that they receive a share of your estate.

Prenuptial Agreements

The topic of prenuptial agreements generally raises a few eyebrows. Many believe that developing a prenuptial agreement dooms a marriage. But a prenuptial agreement can be the right move when one spouse has more assets or earns much more than the other, has substantial debt, has children from a prior marriage who need to be protected in case of death or a second divorce, owns part or all of a business, or is planning to go back to school. (The prenuptial agreement can help ensure that the working partner's contribution to the spouse's education is properly rewarded.)

Taxes

Although some relief from the marriage penalty tax went into effect in 2003, a two-income couple with more than $120,000 of household income still owes more in taxes than two single people with the same total income. So prepare now to pay more to Uncle Sam come April 15.

When you marry, you can choose your filing status; that is, married filing jointly or married filing separately. Discuss your situation with your tax and financial advisor to determine which situation works to your advantage. Usually married filing jointly is the better option. (Chapter 7 discusses taxes in greater detail.)

▶ Map Your Journey: Get Organized!

The first step to getting on track is for you to sit down together and organize your day-to-day financial tasks and routines. The second and perhaps most important step is to organize your essential financial information so that you both know where everything is, in case one of you suddenly becomes ill or has an accident and can't tend to mundane yet critical tasks such as paying the bills.

Although organizing your financial affairs may sound like a daunting task, it really isn't, and it actually saves time and expense in the long run. Here are a few tips to make the process easier.

Start a Basic Home Filing System

Gather all the piles of papers and sort them by the following categories:

▶ Bills due
▶ Important/Keep
▶ Toss/Shred

Then buy colorful file folders and label them for each household expense or activity. If you do not have a file cabinet, buy a plastic file bin or an accordion file. Create one or two files for unpaid bills. As the bills come in, open them, clip the statement to the return envelope, and place them in the "Bills Due" file. Some families create two Bills Due files: one for the first pay period of the month and another for the second pay period.

Create other files, such as receipts and warranties, to be placed with the "Important/Keep" stack of essential household information. Empty both your wallets and photocopy all your credit cards, health cards, and any other cards with information that would be important to have if either of you lost your wallet. Do this task once, then update the file any time there is a change. If you do not want to rent a safety deposit box to hold your important papers, at least keep your valuable information, insurance policies, and passports in a fireproof lock box.

When you bring mail or paperwork into your home, immediately open, review, and sort these items into the three primary categories so that you handle your papers only once. It's said that we spend, on average, six weeks a year looking for misplaced stuff. Imagine how much time you would save if you had a good system in place, not to mention the unnecessary expense of late charges. Consider for a moment that you actually have less time, more frustration, and potentially more expenses because you are disorganized. Invest one or two days in setting up a system, and you will thank yourselves every time you pay bills, pull your tax information together, or need to get your hands on an important document quickly.

Create a Family Financial Binder

Here's another way to organize the most critical information that your spouse would need in event of your death or incapacity. Put all your documents into a single binder. As mentioned previously, many important documents and records should be kept in a safe deposit box or fireproof lock box, especially original or certified copies of birth certificates; Social Security cards; passports; records of adoptions, marriages, and deaths; citizenship and veteran's papers; stock or bond certificates; and insurance policies.

Although you can compile your binder anytime, it's sometimes easier to do it in the first quarter of the year when much of the data arrives for tax preparation purposes. If updated regularly, the binder simplifies many financial tasks, including preparing taxes, obtaining or refinancing loans, and completing other ongoing financial activities. More important, updating the binder allows you to take stock of your economic situation.

You can create the organizer yourself or buy premade ones.

If you do prepare your own organizer, all you need is a large three-ring binder, a three-hole punch, some plastic page protector sheets, and 12 section divider tabs. Make a label with or without a cover sheet so that your binder is clearly identifiable. Create separator pages with index tabs for the following sections: essential personal papers; sources of income; financial assets; deeds and titles; insurance policies; employer-provided benefits; mortgages, loans, and other liabilities; wills, trusts, and other legal documents; advisors/contractors; executor instructions; letters to loved ones; and one marked other.

Once you have the organizer, here are some additional tips.

Decide Who Will Create and Maintain the Binder. The facts in the binder will be invaluable for spouses and adult children who may suddenly take over because of another family member's death or incapacity. It especially makes sense for the spouse who normally does not handle these affairs to be the one to compile the contents of the binder.

Watch Your Mail. As mail comes in, copy the year-end statements from all your financial institutions (banks, mutual fund companies, mortgage lenders, credit cards, insurance companies, and so on). Include year-end pay and benefit statements from employers, pension plans, retirement plans, and the Social Security Administration (your Social Security Benefits Statement will arrive about three months prior to your birthdays). The original will go into your tax return preparation file and then to a safe deposit box. The copy will be inserted into your binder. Make a note of all current beneficiary and transfer-on-death designations for all of these accounts and policies.

Copy All the Important Documents in Your Safe Deposit Box. Make sure to return the originals to the box promptly. Insert the copy into the binder in its proper section, with a notation as to the location of the original document.

Look through Your Wallet. Copy the front and back of your credit cards, health insurance cards, and any other cards with essential information. The idea is to create a paper trail of essential information in case your wallet is lost or stolen.

Tell Appropriate Family Members about the Existence and Location of the Binder. If you like, create a duplicate binder for safekeeping at your office or a loved one's home.

Update the Binder as Information Changes. Here are some suggestions for the types of information that should be included in the binder. You may wish to consider using these headings for the binder's tabs.

1. *Essential personal papers:* Personal and family documents (marriage licenses, divorce papers, birth certificates, adoption papers, and Social Security information)
2. *Sources of income*: Employment or business revenue information, i.e., check stubs, W2s, 1099s
3. *Financial assets:* Investment and related information, i.e., 401(k) statements
4. *Deeds and titles:* Copies of your home, automobiles, or other deeded assets
5. *Insurance policies*: Copies of key pages from your disability, long-term care, automobile, personal life insurance policies, and health insurance policies
6. *Employer-provided benefits:* Copies of health insurance cards, flex spending plan, company disability plan, company-provided life insurance policy, and other work-related benefits
7. *Mortgages, loans, and other liabilities:* Information on your mortgage and other substantial loans (automobile and student loans)
8. *Wills, trusts, and other legal documents*
9. *Advisors/contractors:* Contact information for your attorney and other legal contacts, stockbroker, financial planner or other advisor, insurance broker, CPA or accountant, physician, religious leader, banker, and trust officer. Staple a business card for each advisor to the sheet. This section also may include contractors that provide ongoing home maintenance, pest control, or home security (include copies of contracts).
10. *Executor instructions:* Specifics concerning funeral and obituary information, as well as any other instructions to your executor. You also

may wish to include a list of people to notify in the event of death or an emergency.

11. Letters to loved ones that convey your values and thoughts on life.
12. *Other.* Miscellaneous catchall section.

Taking the time to organize your papers now ensures a more manageable situation if you die or become incapacitated. You will leave a legacy of love and communicate your wishes through your letters and organized plan. You will simplify routine financial tasks and streamline the process for yourself at tax preparation time. The first days of the new year and the annual tax season are excellent times to compile and organize your essential financial information, but *today* is always the best time to get started. Don't let another day go by without starting this important project. Planning pays off!

▶ Prepare for Detours: Establish an Emergency Fund

Preparing an emergency fund should be one of your first financial planning goals. Its purpose is to make sure that you will have cash available when the unexpected happens, such as when the furnace breaks down or an unexpectedly high medical or dental bill not covered by insurance arrives. It's generally much better to use your emergency money than to build up debt on your credit card or borrow money in some other way.

Your emergency fund is just as important when you're married as when you were single. You might think the opposite is true, because when you're married you have another income that you can rely on if one of you can't work because of illness or unemployment. But two can't live exactly as cheaply as one, and if you've been accustomed to living on two incomes, the loss of one will cause not only financial stress but also emotional stress on the partner who will be supporting both of you.

Setting up an emergency fund should be a top priority, but if you have credit card debt or personal loans, *pay those off first.* It does not make sense to carry a credit card balance and pay interest of 9.9 to 21 percent or more while you have cash sitting in a savings account earning 1 percent. Paying off your credit card debt is the best return you can get on your money. Once the credit cards are paid off, use those monthly payments to build up your emergency fund.

What's the Toll? Calculating How Much to Save for Your Emergency Fund

To calculate how much should be in your emergency fund, you first need to consider how well you've covered all of your other financial liabilities. You must think about the amount you spend caring for your dependents (if you have any), the amount of your monthly fixed expenses, the stability of your incomes, your access to low-cost loans, and, the state of the economy and the job market.

A general guideline is that at least three to six months' worth of living expenses should be set aside for an emergency. For example, if you become seriously ill or disabled, there may be a time gap between when your sick pay ends (usually in one to two weeks) and when your long-term disability payments begin (generally after six months). In this case you would need cash to live on for a number of months.

Three to six months' worth of living expenses may be appropriate when your income is secure and the economy and job market are in good shape. But when the economy is uncertain, six months' to a year's worth of living expenses is more suitable. If you get laid off in a poor economy, it could easily take six months (or longer) to find a new job with a comparable income. Unemployment compensation may help for a while, but it is typically no more than 50 percent of your former income and much less if you were highly paid. For example, the maximum unemployment benefit in Massachusetts is about $507 per week (before taxes), which is only about one-quarter of the weekly pretax income of someone who makes $100,000 a year.

There are two ways to estimate how much money should be in your emergency fund. Using the direct method, add all the payments you would need to make in a year even if one of you lost your job (or, if you're really conservative, if *both* of you lost your jobs). These costs would likely include payments on your mortgage, property taxes, insurance, car, credit cards, utilities, groceries, and clothing. Divide the total by 12 for a monthly average, and then multiply the result by three, six, or nine, depending on the number of months of expenses you want to cover. A problem with this approach is that it's easy to overlook some expenditures.

The indirect method leaves less to chance. Most people spend all that they earn. Calculate your monthly income and subtract payroll and income taxes as well as your regular contributions to retirement plans, college savings, and other savings programs. Multiply the result by the number of months you wish to cover. This method is the safest way to estimate your actual spending needs. Whatever the size of your financial cushion, the important thing is to start saving now and do it on a regular basis. Consider having a set amount automatically withdrawn from your checking account every month or every pay period. What you don't see, you'll be less likely to spend.

Planning Even Farther Down the Road

You might also want to prepare for the big expenditures that happen on an irregular basis and estimate their annual cost. Include property taxes and homeowner's insurance premiums (if not escrowed by your mortgage company), auto and life insurance premiums (it is often cheaper to pay annually), anticipated medical and dental bills not covered by insurance, and the costs of projected home maintenance and renovation projects, appliance replacements, vacations, camp for the kids, estimated quarterly income taxes, additional taxes due in April, gifts and holiday spending, and other expenses that you irregularly incur during the year. Add the total and divide by the number of times you pay bills in a year. For example, if you're paid every two weeks, divide by 26. Add this amount for covering irregular expenses to the amount you have decided to set aside in your emergency fund every pay period.

Every time you pay bills, write a check or transfer this irregular expenses amount to your savings account or money market account. Better yet, set up an automatic transfer. What you do not see, you will not spend. When it comes time to pay the car insurance bill, the money will be available, and you will be able to pay it easily.

After you have set this money aside and paid all the bills, you'll know how much you have to live on until the next paycheck arrives. This approach may take some getting used to, especially if what's left doesn't seem like enough. You may need to stop using credit cards until you get a handle on how much you have to spend between paychecks. However, once you make the necessary spending adjustments, you'll know that you're living within your means, saving for a rainy day, and saving for your future. You will be in control of your finances.

Consider regular contributions to your emergency fund as a bill that must be paid. If you receive a tax refund, annual bonus, or other windfall, add that to your savings account instead of spending it.

Make Sure You Can Get There: Keep Your Emergency Fund Accessible

Your emergency fund should be easy to withdraw because this is money you'll need immediately. Therefore, you can't tie up these savings in long-term bonds or stocks; instead, it needs to be accessible.

When starting to build an emergency fund, the best place for it is probably in a savings account where it's FDIC (Federal Deposit Insurance Corporation) insured and is earning a little interest. As you accumulate a few thousand dollars, shop around for higher interest rates in a money market account. Bankrate.com (http://www.bankrate.com) is a good place to look for banks offering savings accounts with the highest rates.

You may want to consider certificates of deposit (CDs), too. If you need the money before the CD matures, you will pay a penalty (typically three to six months' interest). Despite this fact, it might make sense to use a CD for a portion of your emergency fund. Once you have your emergency fund in place, you're ready to move on to the more mundane routine of your financial life: creating a budget.

▶ Share the Driving: Creating a Budget Together

The word *budget* sounds constricting, foreboding, and even a bit frightening. The word has a certain ring to it, vaguely resembling the word *homework* when you were in school. Instead, you should see a budget as your friend. It is the document that gives you control over your finances, in a way that lets you decide what is most and least important to both of you. A budget is an intensely personal plan; there is probably no one you know who has exactly the same priorities you have. If you find it important to include in your budget a lavish ski vacation to the Alps every winter, so be it, as long as the numbers tell you that you can afford it.

Once you become accustomed to budgeting, you will wonder how you got through all these years without one. A budget is a living, breathing document that expands or contracts as your circumstances change. Think of it as a road map, allowing you to know the direction you want to go, but giving you several options on how to get there. For example, you might be planning to buy a house in three years, and you are carefully putting aside money for a down payment. What will happen if you are involved in a car accident that puts you out of work for six months? Your budget must change, causing your down payment plans to be put off for a while. But this does not mean you will never buy the house, just that your budget priorities have had to adapt to altered circumstances.

When you create a budget, you will be able to answer the questions that you have asked yourselves in the past but were never able to resolve conclusively. Here are a few examples:

▶ Do we have enough income to cover the payments if we take on more debt?
▶ Do we have enough money available to cover quarterly tax payments?
▶ Have we put aside enough to cover the holiday presents we want to give?
▶ Will our savings produce enough income to live on and maintain our current lifestyle so we can retire when we want to?
▶ What size mortgage payments can we afford?

Many such questions will continue to arise as you age and move through the different stages of life. The information in your budget worksheet will help you make rational, informed decisions about what you want to do.

Creating a written budget accomplishes several tasks for you. It communicates your priorities in black and white, whereas in the past, you may have only talked about them. The process of making a budget will motivate you to take charge of your financial life. You will feel in control of your money because you will know whether you are spending more or less than you expected. And at the end of your first year with your new budget, you will be able to evaluate how you managed, based on accurate information, making next year's budget even better.

As you create your budget, keep in mind a few common sense tips.

▶ A budget takes thought, so you probably can't do a good job of forecasting all your income and expenses in an afternoon. Plan to do it in several sessions over a week's time.
▶ Begin calculating your budget in pencil so you can erase until all the numbers add up.
▶ Work out a budget *together*. A budget should not be cast in stone. Instead, it should be discussed so you both feel involved in the plan. This way, you have a much better chance of meeting your targets.

- ▶ Be realistic and specific to your situation. Don't count on levels of spending or income that you only wish you had, or that your neighbor has. That will only frustrate the exercise. Also, remember that a budget, by itself, will not increase your income or cut your spending; it will only allow you to see what is going on so you can improve your financial situation.
- ▶ When setting priorities, consider your short-term and long-term financial goals (discussed in detail in the next section) to help you determine what is most and least important to each of you and both of you together.
- ▶ Use round numbers in your budget. It's not necessary to drive yourself crazy by planning your spending to the last penny.
- ▶ When making projections for the next year, don't automatically assume you will earn or spend the same amount in each category as you did the previous year. Last year's figures should be a guide, not a straitjacket. Part of making a budget is taking control of your finances, so increase or decrease the numbers on the expenses side, depending on what you would like to see happen in the next year.

In addition to doing an annual budget, you should keep a running tab of how you are doing on a monthly basis in at least the major categories. A monthly budget will let you compare your budgeted amount with your actual income and spending. It will also help you see the kind of progress you are making toward meeting your budget and which items are furthest from your projections.

Budgeting is such a simple mathematical process, but not enough people take the time to develop and implement a written monthly budget. Even fewer people put these numbers in writing and commit to reviewing them on a regular basis. But without a written budget, you won't know exactly how and where you're currently spending your money. This knowledge is especially important now that you're getting married, and there are two of you trying to keep track of where you're spending your money, both as a couple and individually!

It's no wonder that so many people feel unable to save for their future when they are so totally out of control with their spending. Most investors believe saving and investing are the first steps toward financial independence, but you must first gain control of your spending habits to be able to make room in your budget for savings. If you step back and reflect on what frustrates you most about managing your money, the feeling of chaos will rank at the top of the list for most people. Yet if you take the time to bring some order to your spending, you will find more security in your day-to-day living.

Look in Your Rearview Mirror: Find Out Where Your Money Is Spent

One really easy way to get a sense of where your money is going is to use "the checkbook method," in which you go through your checkbook and credit card statements for the previous year and fit every transaction into the appropriate budget category. For example, see Roadmap 1.1, which shows how one couple spent their money last year. They have a combined income of $120,000 per year. Notice that they wanted to increase savings and had worked hard to pay off the balance on their credit cards.

The key to your success is putting your budget in writing and monitoring your spending on a regular basis. You must be realistic when preparing your personal budget goals. If you are attempting to increase your savings, then increase them slowly. If you are attempting to reduce your overall spending, then look at the numbers and create a budget that is attainable. Roadmap 1.2 is a blank version of a form that you can use to create your own checkbook test.

Once you have every transaction listed on a form like Roadmap 1.2 or on a spreadsheet, it's easy to see where you're spending your money and to create a 12-month budget for the next year. This process is a task you and your spouse should do together: It helps you understand the past and current choices you are making with your income. And it allows you to make decisions about how you plan for the future.

Very few people know where their money is actually going. They may comment, "We have a general idea of how we spend it." But when they take the checkbook test, many people are surprised by the amount of money they spend on unbudgeted items.

Check Your Side Mirrors: What Expenditures Are Overtaking You?

If you are looking for places to reduce your monthly outflows, you may want to review expenditures that are "money magnets." Many purchases are money magnets: the little payments that seem so insignificant that you swear you'll never miss the money. But at the end of the month, you may be surprised

"The Checkbook Method" Shows Where You Spend Your Money

Month	Last Year's Actual	This Year's Goal	This Year's Actual
Personal Savings/Investments	250	350	
Retirement Investments	833	833	
Mortgage/Rent	1200	1200	
Electric Utility	200	200	
Gas Utility	50	50	
Telephone/Other Phone Costs	75	75	
Cell Phone	50	50	
Pager	20	20	
Water	25	25	
Cable TV	33	33	
Home Maintenance	150	150	
Lawn Maintenance	50	50	
Real Estate Taxes			
Car Payment	340	340	
Car Insurance	200	200	
Gasoline	125	125	
Car Maintenance	20	20	
Food/Groceries	700	700	
Toiletries			
Eating Out	400	400	
Entertainment	100	100	
Clothing	200	200	
Vacations	200	200	
Childcare/Dependent Care	300	300	
Tuition			

Category			
Visa	250	0	
MasterCard	75	0	
Discover			
Other Consumer Debt			
Student Loans			
Homeowners Insurance			
Health Insurance			
Life Insurance	100	100	
Disability Insurance	50	50	
Doctors—Co-payments	35	35	
Dentists	15	15	
Eyeglasses	15	15	
Prescription Drugs	25	25	
Household Help	175	175	
Dry Cleaning	125	125	
Beauty Salon/Barber	41	41	
Pets/Vet			
Subscriptions	20	20	
Florists	20	20	
Gifts	300	300	
Religious Donations	1000	1000	
Community Donations	50	50	
Art/Dance/Misc. Personal	30	30	
CPA	30	30	
Professional Dues			
Club Dues	45	45	
Miscellaneous	200	200	
Other			
Totals	$8,122	$7,897	

Blank Checkbook Spreadsheet

Month							Monthly Subtotal
Personal Savings/Investments							
Retirement Investments							
Mortgage/Rent							
Electric Utility							
Gas Utility							
Telephone/Other Phone Costs							
Cell Phone							
Pager							
Water							
Cable TV							
Home Maintenance							
Lawn Maintenance							
Real Estate Taxes							
Car Payment							
Car Insurance							
Gasoline							
Car Maintenance							
Food/Groceries							
Toiletries							
Eating Out							
Entertainment							
Clothing							
Vacations							
Childcare/Dependent Care							
Tuition							

Visa									
MasterCard									
Discover									
Other Consumer Debt									
Student Loans									
Homeowners Insurance									
Health Insurance									
Life Insurance									
Disability Insurance									
Doctors—Co-payments									
Dentists									
Eyeglasses									
Prescription Drugs									
Household Help									
Dry Cleaning									
Beauty Salon/Barber									
Pets/Vet									
Subscriptions									
Florists									
Gifts									
Religious Donations									
Community Donations									
Art/Dance/Misc. Personal									
CPA									
Professional Dues									
Club Dues									
Miscellaneous									
Other									
Monthly Total									

1. A large house
2. Large car payments
3. Too much personal debt
4. Large cell phone bills
5. Clothes
6. Dining out
7. Overspending on holiday and birthday presents

when you add up all these expenses. Tollbooth 1.1 shows a typical list of big money magnets, but even more insidious are some common small money magnets listed in Tollbooth 1.2.

This list of small money magnets alone adds up to a whopping $445 per month! You can see how these items are like magnets: They pull money out of your budget, but because each expense is such a small amount, you are unaware of the overall impact as it is occurring. Assuming you both are willing to review the small money magnets in your budget, would saving and investing this amount of money make any difference in your financial future? Obviously, it's important to have a clear understanding of where your money is going. You may want to review your big money magnets before moving on.

Why not take the checkbook test to see how you are spending your money? Like many people, you may wonder how you are currently making ends meet even though you are committed to making your money begin to work for you. Once you know what you've actually spent during the previous year, you can create a budget worksheet and input the actual figures from last year and goals for the new year, as shown in Roadmap 1.3. Beside the goals is a blank line that lets you track your actual spending on a month-by-month basis. Your goal should be to stay at or below last year's expenses or to reduce the amounts in some areas.

Finally, remember that you only have so much money coming in after taxes, and there are definite limits on how far that money can be stretched. It is critical that you, as a couple, commit to a plan for your future. It boils down to choices and simple math. If you make $50,000 after taxes, you must plan to spend less than $50,000. If you make $100,000 after taxes, you must

Tollbooth 1.2

Small "Money Magnets"

1. Eating out at lunch	$5.00 × 20 days = $100
2. Snacks at work	$1.00 × 20 days = $ 20
3. Soft drinks at work	$2.00 × 20 days = $ 40
4. Yogurt/ice cream for family	$4.00 × 5 days = $ 20
5. Gum	$0.50 × 10 days = $ 5
6. Internet connection	$ 25
7. Extra phone line for Internet	$ 24
8. Call waiting	$ 5
9. Caller ID	$ 5
10. Cell phone	$ 50
11. Subscriptions to magazines/newspapers	$ 20
12. CDs (one per month)	$ 14
13. Movie rentals (one per week)	$3.00 × 4 = $ 12
14. Impulse purchases at the grocery store	$ 25
15. Recreation—golf/tennis/aerobics	$ 50
16. Pets—food/grooming	$ 30
Total per month:	$445!

plan to spend less than $100,000. The ability to succeed rests on the choices you make for spending your money.

Budgeting is one of the few areas of financial planning over which you have total control. If your budget is out of line, you can start taking steps today to bring it back in line; once again, a matter of choices and simple math. Here's the simple equation to begin your budget.

$$\text{Expenses} < \text{Income}$$

Where can you find a little extra money in your budget? Then what will you do with that extra money? Pay off debt? Invest for your children's future? Put it aside for an emergency fund? Begin to save for your next car, so you will be able to pay cash? Fund your 401(k)? The budgeting process puts you ahead of the game instead of behind it. The budget allows you to make decisions ahead of time rather than reacting to unforeseen circumstances after they happen. Today is the day to begin!

Roadmap 1.3

Sample Budget Worksheet

	Month 1	Month 2	Yearly Average
Personal Savings/Investments	_____	_____	_____
Retirement Investments	_____	_____	_____
Mortgage	_____	_____	_____
Electric Utility	_____	_____	_____
Gas Utility	_____	_____	_____
Telephone	_____	_____	_____
Cell Phone(s)	_____	_____	_____
Water	_____	_____	_____
Cable TV	_____	_____	_____
Home Maintenance	_____	_____	_____
Lawn Maintenance	_____	_____	_____
Real Estate Taxes	_____	_____	_____
Personal Property Taxes	_____	_____	_____
Car Payment	_____	_____	_____
Car Insurance	_____	_____	_____
Gasoline	_____	_____	_____
Car Maintenance	_____	_____	_____
Food (Groceries/Dining Out)	_____	_____	_____
Toiletries	_____	_____	_____
Clothing	_____	_____	_____
Entertainment	_____	_____	_____
Visa/Amex/MasterCard/Loans	_____	_____	_____
Vacations	_____	_____	_____

	Month 1	Month 2	Yearly Average
Childcare/Dependent Care	_____	_____	_____
Tuition	_____	_____	_____
Homeowners Insurance	_____	_____	_____
Health Insurance	_____	_____	_____
Life Insurance	_____	_____	_____
Disability Insurance	_____	_____	_____
Doctors	_____	_____	_____
Dentists	_____	_____	_____
Eyeglasses	_____	_____	_____
Medications	_____	_____	_____
Household Help	_____	_____	_____
Dry Cleaning	_____	_____	_____
Beauty Salon/Barber	_____	_____	_____
Pets/Vets	_____	_____	_____
Subscriptions	_____	_____	_____
Gifts	_____	_____	_____
Religious Donations	_____	_____	_____
Community Donations	_____	_____	_____
Lessons/Hobbies	_____	_____	_____
Professional Advisors (CPA, CFP, Attorney, Tax Preparer)	_____	_____	_____
Professional Dues	_____	_____	_____
Miscellaneous	_____	_____	_____
Other Club Dues	_____	_____	_____
Other	_____	_____	_____
MONTHLY TOTAL	_____	_____	_____

▶ Where Do You Want to Go? Defining Your Financial Goals

Once you have a budget to manage your daily, monthly, and annual expenses, you should think about your financial goals, for the short term as well as the long term. Before you can begin the process of writing your financial goals, though, it's important to understand your *life* goals. It's easy to get lost in the numbers if you don't know exactly what you are trying to accomplish. You must know what your ultimate objectives are; for example, do you want to

1. increase your current standard of living?
2. save for your children's education?
3. enjoy a secure retirement?

Sit down together and decide what you want and need from your financial plan. The more definite you can be in setting your objectives and goals, the more likely that you will be able to create a realistic and satisfactory plan for your financial future. If you're planning to drive to a distant destination, you would probably create a detailed and specific itinerary, especially if you're unfamiliar with the area. Your written goals should be equally well-planned.

You can quickly and easily begin to quantify every financial goal—exactly how much money is required for everything from family vacations and your children's college education to your retirement. However, you must understand these calculations are simply hypothetical illustrations of what might happen. It is impossible to know the rate of return that your savings and investments will actually earn or the inflation rate that will diminish their value. But that should not keep you from being excited about attempting to quantify the dreams you have for yourself and your family.

Quantifying your personal goals and putting them on a specific timeline can bring great freedom to your saving and spending habits. Some people are not saving enough and some people may be saving too much. Wouldn't it be nice to know that you are on track? For many investors, this step is where budgeting decisions have to be made. Consider these typical questions that young couples ask:

▶ How are we going to be able to save $100 a month for our child's education?

▶ How will we set aside $4,000 a year for each of our IRAs and where will we find the funds for our 401(k) plans?

▶ Where can we find the $400 a month to replace our car in four years?

Although everyone's questions will be different, now is the time to review your monthly budget and establish priorities for how you are going to spend your income. Some people complete the budgeting process and realize that they do not have enough income to cover their regular monthly bills and the additional savings needed for a child's education or an IRA contribution. Budgeting can be one of the most challenging areas of financial planning, but if you begin to gain some control over your personal spending and shift that money into personal savings, you will be closer to attaining your goals and you will feel a tremendous sense of accomplishment.

Create a *Written* Map: It's Important to Write Down Your Financial Goals

One study on goals indicates that 87 percent of people have not taken the time to set goals for themselves, 10 percent have goals but have not yet written them down, and only 3 percent have written goals. The same study concluded that the 3 percent who actually take the time and effort to put their goals in writing accomplish 50 to 100 times more than people who have not established written goals and objectives.

Writing your goals can be viewed as a turning point for your personal financial plan. Roadmap 1.4 is a short list of common financial goals. Check the ones you hope to accomplish, and include a start date and a finish date beside each goal. Now circle your goals in each category. Write some or all of your goals on a card and look at your goals often; they should serve as a reminder that you need to be committed to doing the day-to-day activities that will help you to reach your goals.

Now break your goals into manageable parts. Set timelines to review your progress. Share your goals with each other, remembering that each partner should contribute to working toward your goals.

What's Your ETA? Create a Timeline for Achieving Your Goals

Quantifying your goals is incredibly important, but it's also necessary to create a realistic timeline. Your timeline allows you to plot your financial future and choose the goals you plan to fund. Your timeline and a quantified

Roadmap 1.4

Common Financial Goals

Investment Goals	Start	Finish
Plan for retirement	_____	_____
Educate children or grandchildren	_____	_____
Accumulate a nest egg	_____	_____
Increase income	_____	_____
Reduce debt	_____	_____
Plan for a second home	_____	_____
Reduce taxes	_____	_____
Increase monthly investment amount	_____	_____

Personal Financial Goals	Start	Finish
Increase financial knowledge	_____	_____
Create a family budget	_____	_____
Learn how to read newspaper financial quotes	_____	_____
Learn how to read financial statements	_____	_____
Read more	_____	_____
Join or start an investment club	_____	_____

goal sheet, which lists the funds you will need to achieve each goal, will allow you to calculate the total amount of money needed to fulfill your future financial plan. Your timeline and goal sheet will also help you to rank your priorities and fund them accordingly. For example:

- ▶ college education—$120,000—needed by 2025
- ▶ retirement planning—$750,000—needed by 2045
- ▶ vacation home—$200,000—wanted by 2010

These goals may seem daunting, but when they are broken down into manageable pieces and you start to fund them on a regular basis, you will be amazed at how many goals you can reach. Setting specific financial objectives and putting them in writing by listing the dollar amounts and noting exactly when you will need the money will motivate you to achieve your goals. Many people never take the time to figure out what they want because they have convinced themselves that they will never reach their targets. If you don't define your goals, you won't accomplish them.

This section will give you several easy-to-complete worksheets so you will be able to determine your top financial priorities and how you can achieve them. You can't reach all your goals overnight, but knowing what they are and which ones take precedence will help you fulfill your goals faster than if you never took the time to do this exercise. Because setting goals is really another way of defining priorities, the process helps you make sure that your limited resources and income are used most effectively to attain your highest priorities. By crystallizing your aspirations, you take charge of your life so that you control your money for the purposes you find most important.

Don't think that goal setting is too hard; you've been doing it for most of your life. When you last started a diet, you set a specific goal of the number of pounds you would trim. When you were on the track team in high school, you set a goal to achieve a particular time for your event: a four-minute mile, for instance. During college, you set a goal to attain a specific grade point average or a record that would enable you to enter a certain graduate school. All you are doing now is applying the same discipline to your personal finances.

Remember, setting goals is not only about allocating your money, it's also about allocating your time. If one of your goals is to have more free time to play with your children or do community work, the time spent reaching that goal will limit the time you can devote to advancing your career. Nothing is wrong with that choice as long as it is one you make consciously.

Because you're sharing your finances with your spouse, goal setting must be done mutually. To avoid friction between you, you must agree, for the most part, with your spouse or significant other on which goals get high priority. You can avoid many financial fights by coming to terms on goals at the beginning of the process.

The goal-setting exercises in Roadmaps 1.5 through 1.9 are not once-in-a-lifetime events. As you accomplish certain goals during your life, you must constantly set new ones. For example, once your children's college educations have been paid, you may want to shift priorities and set aside money for a second home or your retirement.

There are three kinds of goals: short-term, medium-term, and long-term. Within each of these three categories, you not only have goals but also priorities for these goals. Because it's likely you won't have enough money to achieve all your goals over the next year, you have to allocate some resources on an ongoing basis to each of the three categories so that you have some chance of accomplishing your goals over time. Usually people neglect the medium- and long-term goals in favor of the seemingly more pressing short-term goals, but that only puts off the day of reckoning, when the time to pay for college or retirement comes.

The longer you delay accumulating the money for your long-term goals, such as buying a home or funding retirement, the more difficult it will be for you to realize those goals. This section provides a worksheet for each of the three kinds of goals. After you locate one of your goals on the worksheet, note the amount of money you will need to pay for it, how high a priority it is compared to your other goals, and when you would like to achieve it.

Short-Term Goals: These are goals you would like to achieve within the next year. They might include paying off your credit cards; buying large items, such as a television, car, or furniture; or taking a much-needed vacation. Roadmap 1.5 is a worksheet to help both of you determine your short-term goals.

Medium-Term Goals: These goals include items that require between two and 10 years to accumulate the money needed, such as building a down payment for a first or second home, creating a college fund for children older than eight years, or saving up to take the overseas trip of your dreams. If you're planning on having a child in a few years, you might want to start

Roadmap 1.5

Short-Term Goals Worksheet

Goal	Priority	Date to Accomplish	$ Amount Needed
Build up Emergency Reserve (worth three months' salary)	_____	_____	_____
Buy Adequate Insurance	_____	_____	_____
Auto	_____	_____	_____
Health	_____	_____	_____
Home	_____	_____	_____
Life	_____	_____	_____
Contribute to Charity Name _____	_____	_____	_____
Fund IRA or Keogh Account	_____	_____	_____
Increase Contribution to Company Benefit Plan	_____	_____	_____
Join a Health/Sports Club	_____	_____	_____
Make Major Home Improvements	_____	_____	_____
Make Major Purchases	_____	_____	_____
Pay Off Bills	_____	_____	_____
Pay Off Credit Cards	_____	_____	_____
Save for Holiday Gifts, Birthdays, etc.	_____	_____	_____
Take Vacation	_____	_____	_____
Other (specify) _____	_____	_____	_____
TOTAL $ AMOUNT NEEDED			$ _____

putting aside money for the little one now. After all, economists project that it will cost at least $300,000 to bring up a child from birth through the senior year in high school (assuming you are able to exert some control over the child's demands for toys in the early years and high-fashion clothing in the teen years). Roadmap 1.6 provides a worksheet to help you think about your medium-term goals.

Long-Term Goals: These goals take more than 10 years to fulfill. The most common long-term goal is a financially secure retirement, which takes a lifetime of financial discipline. Other long-term goals include paying for extensive travel, starting your own business, going back to school to receive a higher degree of education, and buying a vacation home. Another long-term goal is to make sure you can afford medical care in your later years. Roadmap 1.7 provides a worksheet to help you think about your long-term goals.

Following Mile Markers: Calculating Monthly Savings Needed to Reach Your Goals

To figure out the monthly amount you need to invest to reach each goal you've listed on any of the previous worksheets, use the table in Tollbooth 1.3. The left column shows the number of years remaining until you need the money for your goal. The next four columns show the divisors (numbers to use in calculations) for four different rates of return that you may assume it is possible to earn on average over a long period of time. These rates of return assume you have adjusted for the effects of inflation and taxes, so they are known by the term *real after-tax yields*. The higher the rate of return, the more risk you have to take in your investment choices to achieve it.

To use the table in Tollbooth 1.3, take the amount of money you will need to pay for your goal and pick an assumed rate of return. Then find the divisor for the number of years you have allocated to reach the goal. Simply divide your dollar goal by the divisor, and you have figured out the monthly amount of savings you need to reach your goal. The divisor automatically calculates the effect of the compounding of interest, which becomes quite a powerful force over time.

For example, let's say you want to accumulate a $100,000 nest egg for your retirement in 20 years. Let's also assume that you'll receive a real after-tax yield of 6 percent. When you look down the 6 percent column to the 20-year line, you see the divisor of 462. Divide $100,000 by 462, and you'll find that you'll have to save $216.45 a month to meet your goal.

Roadmap 1.6

Medium-Term Goals Worksheet

Goal	Priority	Date to Accomplish	$ Amount Needed
Create College Fund for Children			
Child 1 _____	_____	_____	_____
Child 2 _____	_____	_____	_____
Save Down Payment for First Home	_____	_____	_____
Save Down Payment for Second Home	_____	_____	_____
Finance Special Occasions (weddings, bar mitzvahs, etc.)	_____	_____	_____
Help Child Finance Home	_____	_____	_____
Pay Off Education Debt	_____	_____	_____
Save for Next Child	_____	_____	_____
Take Overseas Trip	_____	_____	_____
Take Time off to Pursue an Interest	_____	_____	_____
Other (specify)			
_____	_____	_____	_____
TOTAL $ NEEDED			$_____

Roadmap 1.7

Long-Term Goals Worksheet

Goal	Priority	Date to Accomplish	$ Amount Needed
Buy Retirement Home	_____	_____	_____
Buy Vacation Home	_____	_____	_____
Continue Education	_____	_____	_____
Contribute to Charity	_____	_____	_____
Establish Long-Term Health Care for Self and/or Spouse	_____	_____	_____
Establish Retirement Fund	_____	_____	_____
Help Older Parents	_____	_____	_____
Make a Charitable Bequest	_____	_____	_____
Pay Off Mortgage Early	_____	_____	_____
Start a Business	_____	_____	_____
Start a Second Career	_____	_____	_____
Travel Extensively	_____	_____	_____
Other (specify)			
_____	_____	_____	_____
TOTAL $ NEEDED			$_____

Tollbooth 1.3

Determining the Monthly Savings Needed to Reach a Goal

	Divisors (By Rate of Return)		
Years to Goal	2%	4%	6%
1	12.1	12.2	12.3
2	24.5	24.9	25.4
3	37.1	38.2	39.3
4	49.9	51.9	54.1
5	63.1	66.2	69.8
6	76.5	81.1	86.4
7	90.2	96.6	104.1
8	104.2	112.7	122.8
9	118.4	129.5	142.7
10	133.0	146.9	163.9
11	147.8	165.1	186.3
12	163.0	184.0	210.1
13	178.5	203.6	235.4
14	194.2	224.0	262.3
15	210.4	245.3	290.8
16	226.8	267.4	321.1
17	243.6	290.4	353.2
18	260.7	314.3	387.3
19	278.2	339.2	423.6
20	296.1	365.1	462.0
21	314.2	392.1	502.9
22	332.8	420.1	546.2
23	351.8	449.3	592.2
24	371.2	479.6	641.1
25	390.9	511.2	693.0

Here's an example of a short-term goal. Let's say you need $2,000 in two years to buy furniture for your living room. Assuming a 2 percent rate of return, you divide $2,000 by the divisor of 24.5 to come up with a monthly savings target of $81.63. That's not so difficult. Now that you've clearly defined your short-term, medium-term, and long-term goals, you should be feeling better already!

A New Destination

If You're Buying a Home

Nearly 5 million people buy new and existing homes in the United States each year, and for many of them, it's their first home purchase. Almost two-thirds of this group are married, and most have spent between two and five years saving for a down payment. Most will buy a single-family home, with the remainder buying townhouses, condos, or co-ops. This chapter will help you with one of the biggest financial commitments you and your spouse will likely make: buying a home and figuring out how to pay for it.

Before we get into the nitty gritty, keep in mind that for some people who are getting married, renting may be advantageous. You pay no maintenance, property taxes, or repair costs. Financial experts estimate that for every dollar a homeowner spends to buy a home, they spend $1.50 on interest, repairs, maintenance, property taxes, and other costs.

If you and your spouse rent, you can save or invest the money that a homeowner would spend on a new roof, property taxes, or landscaping. Nevertheless, you or your spouse may feel that the return on a home investment is an incentive to own rather than rent. So let's do the math. A typical down payment is 20 percent of the home's value. For a $150,000 purchase, that's $30,000. If the value of that same home increases 2 percent next year to $153,000, the return (not counting taxes) is more than 2 percent because of the leverage from the down payment. Divide the $3,000 that represents the home's increase in value by the $30,000 down payment. You are left with a 10 percent return on your home investment.

▶ Cut to the Chase: Can You Afford to Buy a Home?

You and your spouse need to feel comfortable that you can afford to buy a home. Don't make the mistake of thinking that your only housing expense will be your mortgage payment. Homeowners face costs that renters do not. You'll need to pay for the following:

- ▶ mortgage (more about this soon)
- ▶ taxes
- ▶ insurance
- ▶ maintenance
- ▶ homeowners' fees for a condo, co-op, or association
- ▶ all utilities

Now that you know what the basic expenses will be, consider your specific financial situation. Let's make a quick U-turn and review the basic financial information you compiled in Chapter 1 when you created your budget and in Roadmap 1.3, in which you listed your expenses. Once you've done that, we can build on that map and provide a clearer estimate. Tollbooth 2.1 provides an easy way to calculate how much you and your spouse will be able to pay. It converts your current rent into what you could afford to pay for a mortgage.

But you need to know more than how a mortgage will compare to rent. There are three basic financial questions:

1. How much money can we afford to pay for a home?
2. How big a monthly payment can we afford?
3. How much money will we need to pay for the down payment?

You will need to answer these questions before you can seriously go house hunting. It's a waste of time, effort, and hope to look at homes in the $200,000 to $250,000 range when you can only afford $75,000 to $150,000. It's important to know what you can afford before you invest too much shoe leather, miles per gallon, and daydreaming in finding a perfect home that you can't pay for.

Tollbooth 2.1

Can You Afford to Buy a Home?
Monthly Rent vs. a Mortgage Payment

The following formula arbitrarily assumes that 10 percent of your mythical mortgage payment will cover homeowners insurance and the repayment of the principal, with the rest paying deductible interest and property taxes. It also assumes that your top tax bracket (known to accountants as your *marginal tax rate*) is 28 percent. If your tax bracket is higher, your tax savings will be correspondingly higher.

A.	Your present rent	$ _____
B.	Multiply by 1.32	× 1.32
C.	Equivalent monthly mortgage payment	$ _____

The result (line C) is a rough estimate of the amount you can spend on a monthly mortgage payment, including the principal, interest, property taxes, and homeowners insurance, without owing any more money at the end of the income tax year than you would have by renting.

General mortgage qualification guidelines state that you can spend up to 28 percent of your monthly gross pretax income for housing (front-end ratio), and that the monthly cost of all debt, including housing, cannot exceed 33 percent (back-end ratio). First-time buyers need to be aware of these guidelines because they often get loans with a a down payment of 10 percent or less that leaves them with too much debt.

▶ Getting Started and Passing "Go": Getting Preapproval for a Mortgage

In the past, accurate information about purchasing a home was often difficult to come by. A real estate agent might tell you one thing, a seller might tell you something else, and a friend who seemed to know something about real estate might have another answer altogether. Fortunately, now you can quickly, easily, and, *accurately* answer your financial homebuying questions. And in the process, you can also acquire a tool that may allow you to leverage a better price. The tool is called "preapproval."

To get preapproved, you go through the process of applying for a mortgage from an actual lender before you've found a home. You fill out an application and put up a fee (usually under $50) for a credit report. The lender will look at your application and determine how much money you have available for a down payment, what your income is, and how solid your credit history looks. The section "What to Pack" lists the information you should be prepared to provide when applying for preapproval of a mortgage.

The lender will also look at your credit history and how long you have lived at your present address. The creditor will verify your length of residence by contacting your landlord or mortgage lender. Whether you pay your rent or mortgage on time is reviewed closely because it may indicate how you will pay your new loan.

If you are up front about any credit problems, many creditors will work with you or show you what to do to reapply in the future. This is no time for you or your spouse to be shy or embarrassed about finances because everything will come out sooner or later. It's better to be fully informed before you waste a lot of time looking at something unobtainable. Lenders use a formula to determine what percentage of your income you can afford to allocate toward purchasing a home. They also take a close look at your credit rating,

What to Pack

Here's the information you need to provide to get preapproved for a mortgage:

- ▶ Recent paycheck stub
- ▶ Two years of income tax forms if you're self-employed
- ▶ Verification of deposit from your bank showing that you have the necessary down payment on account. The lender will likely have to sign the document and send it out directly to the lender. Sometimes your bankbook or copies of account balance statements alone will do.
- ▶ Verification of employment from your employer showing how long you've been employed and stating your chances for continued employment. The lender will likely have to sign the document and will send it to your employer directly. Some lenders verify employment with just a phone call.
- ▶ Any other documents the lender may need, such as proof that you've paid off an old loan that shows up unpaid in a credit report.

which is why it's so important to take care of your credit. It's not something you can build or rebuild overnight.

Check Your Speed Limit: What Your FICO Score Says about Your Credit

When you apply for a mortgage, your credit report is obtained. Lenders are interested in what your FICO score is: This is a credit-scoring system developed by Fair, Isaac & Company (hence, FICO) that is used by many lenders to determine a borrower's ability to repay a mortgage. The FICO system uses a scoring range of 300–850. A score is based on the information listed in your credit report. The score measures the degree of risk that your loan will represent to the lender. The lower your score, the higher the risk you are to the lender.

The score doesn't include your income, assets, or bank accounts. It isn't calculated by using age, sex, race, color, religion, marital status, occupation, homeownership status, length of time at present address, or zip codes. FICO score models (methods of computing scores) are available through the three national credit reporting agencies: Experian, Trans Union, and Equifax. The numbers produced by all three models are often referred to as FICO scores. The names of the scoring programs at the three bureaus are: Beacon at Equifax, Empirica at Trans Union, and Fair Isaac Model at Experian.

FICO scores range from approximately 300 to 850 points. Acceptable scores can vary according to the type of credit you are trying to obtain. Scores fall into four categories:

1. *750 or above.* You are considered the cream of the crop.
2. *700 to 749.* Okay but room for improvement.
3. *620 to 699.* You are in a questionable category. This doesn't mean you won't be approved, but you will have to provide more documentation to the lender to satisfy its requirements and you'll pay a higher interest rate.
4. *Below 620.* You may get a loan, but you'll pay *a lot more* interest than someone with a higher score.

When a credit report is sought for a married couple by a credit grantor for purposes of qualifying for a line of credit, the husband and wife will each have a FICO score because they are not viewed as one entity. Very seldom will both husband and wife have the same score. When qualifying jointly for a mortgage, the individual who has the highest income is the one whose score will count the most toward a loan approval. Also, keep in mind that a person who has a perfect credit report with no negative information can still receive a low FICO score by having too much debt.

There can be different FICO scores from each of the three credit reporting agencies. To find out why you received a particular FICO score, look at the four codes next to the score. An explanation for the score, consisting of the top four reasons in order of severity, is printed underneath the codes.

It is important to know what your FICO score is; however, the only way you can find your score is by asking a credit grantor to tell you. You will not receive your score when you request your credit report from any of the three credit reporting agencies.

Improving a Low FICO Score. If you find out that your FICO score is too low to get the best interest rates offered, you can improve your score and try to apply at a later date. Here are some ideas on how to raise your FICO score:

▶ Review your past payment history on your credit report. Bankruptcies, foreclosures, collection accounts, and delinquencies will cost you many points. Contact the credit bureaus about any incorrect or inaccurate entries on your report. Do this before you apply for credit. Your payment record carries the most weight on your score.

▶ Keep in mind that scores are lower for consumers with no bank credit cards or those with five or more bank credit cards. Two to four cards are a good balance. If you decide to close any accounts, do not close your oldest accounts. The longer you have held an account, the better it is for your score.

▶ Keep your balances well below their credit limit. The amount of debt you carry on your credit cards and other accounts is the second biggest factor in determining your score. If your total debt is more than 75 percent of the total credit limits, your score will suffer.

▶ Avoid frequent inquiries from lenders. According to the score models, the risk of default appears to rise after two to four inquiries within six to 12 months. Inquiries are not picked up when consumers check their own credit report.

▶ Try not to open several new credit card accounts or take out loans over a short period because this can hurt your score. If you have high balances on those new cards, your score will be lowered. Have one or two lines of new credit established within the past two years maximum.

▶ Keep in mind that recent negative entries on your credit report are worse than problems that occurred years ago. An account that has been delinquent in the past six months will hurt you more than a bankruptcy five years ago. It appears that problems more than two years old won't hurt your score as much as those that are more recent.

▶ Avoid obtaining loans from finance companies because this will also lower your credit score. Finance companies, often used as a last resort by people who need cash, charge extremely high interest rates.

If you are having problems paying your bills, prioritize them to avoid severe damage to your credit report. Pay your mortgage first, then your car payment, followed by payments on your credit cards and other revolving

---

Hazard!
Make Sure Your Credit Reports Are Up To Date

When you apply for a mortgage, the mortgage company will run "a standard factual" report on you. This document combines information from the three credit bureaus: Experian (TRW), Trans Union, and Equifax. It's part of the qualification that underwriters look for to approve a loan.

Errors are frequently found in these reports. If a negative entry surfaces, the mortgage company will either ask you for a letter of explanation or contact the creditor who is reporting the entry to verify it. If it's incorrect, the creditor will submit a letter acknowledging their error and correct it.

This correction can help you get approval for your mortgage, but most of the time, the original credit bureaus have not been notified by the creditor. If the error has not been deleted from their system, it can reappear on your credit report. Therefore, you need to send a copy of the creditor's letter to the mortgage company, as well as a letter to each credit bureau, asking them to update their files.

Always check your credit reports from all three bureaus, or get a three-in-one report, before you apply for a mortgage. By doing this, you can solve any problems before you make an application and risk being denied credit.

---

accounts. Don't make partial payments unless the credit grantor agrees to it and will not report the payments as late.

Once you have tried to raise your FICO score, wait four to six weeks before reapplying for your loan. It takes at least that long to have the creditors update your credit files. Have your loan officer run another credit report to see the results. If the FICO score is still too low, continue to find ways to improve it.

Don't allow several creditors to obtain inquiries about your credit before you have requested your credit report directly from the credit reporting agencies. Make sure that there are no problems that need to be corrected before you apply for a mortgage.

Check Your Rearview Mirror: If You've Filed for Bankruptcy

If you or your spouse have filed for bankruptcy in the past, it's still possible to get a mortgage. There are a few lenders who will give you a home loan but you would have to go through a mortgage broker who has access to different lenders offering these programs.

There is a question in the mortgage loan application that will ask you if you have ever filed for bankruptcy. It is important that you inform the loan officer about your situation before you apply. A bankruptcy is a public notice, so if for some reason it is not on your credit report, it is filed at the county recorder's office, and it could easily be revealed. Have the lender prequalify you before you look for a home.

The lender wants to see that you have been able to reestablish good credit since your bankruptcy. Job stability, the size of your income, and the amount of your down payment will play an important role in your qualification.

Back on Track: What the Preapproval Letter Tells You

From all the information you and your spouse have provided, the lender determines the maximum loan you can get. This amount tells you how much house you can qualify for, unless you can add money you've stashed under the mattress, or you've made a killing in the stock market, or you're getting help with the down payment from your family. After the underwriters approve, you get a letter stating that you are preapproved for the loan.

Your preapproval letter may state that you can borrow up to a certain amount of money at a specific interest rate. Or it may state that you are preapproved for a maximum monthly payment. Lenders prefer to name a maximum monthly payment. The reason is that although the largest monthly payment you can afford to make won't change, interest rates will. As interest rates go up, your maximum loan amount will go down. As interest rates go down, your maximum loan amount will go up.

The preapproval letter is something both you and a home seller can bank on, literally. It is a commitment from a lender to loan you and your spouse money. It says that if the property you wish to buy is of appropriate value and if your financial situation doesn't change, you *will* get financing. The lender stands behind you.

In short, preapproval will tell you

▶ your maximum monthly payment,
▶ your maximum loan,
▶ your minimum down payment.

With the preapproval process completed, you will know how much you and your spouse can qualify for to pay for a home! That means you can now devote yourselves to the next stage of buying a home.

Detour: Another Advantage of Preapproval

You can also use your preapproval letter to motivate sellers. Consider their position: They want a good price for their home, but they also know that most buyers must get a mortgage in order to purchase. This situation introduces uncertainty. Will you, the buyers, be able to get a mortgage large enough to make the purchase? Oftentimes the sellers don't know whether the sale can be completed until after the buyers have spent a few weeks getting a mortgage and all parties have signed a sales agreement. On the other hand, when you're preapproved, it's a sure thing. You've already been to a lender. The lender has already said yes. What's there to be uncertain about? When you're competing against buyers who don't have preapproval, you're the one most likely to win the deal. And when you're offering a lower price than the seller is asking, you're more likely to get your offer accepted, all because you have preapproval.

Getting a preapproval letter is the best way to determine how big a mortgage and how big a house you can afford. And it's also a good way to get a better deal.

A Better Road: Preapproval for a Mortgage Beats Being "Prequalified"

On your journey toward preapproval, you or your spouse may hear someone speak of getting you "prequalified" (or simply "qualified"). Don't be misled. Prequalification is nothing more than receiving a statement of opinion. The opinion can be given by anyone and simply states that you are likely to get a mortgage for a certain amount.

In the past real estate agents frequently prequalified their buyers with an oral statement of their financial worthiness. In truth, however, no one stands behind a prequalification. As far as savvy buyers and sellers are concerned, it's of little value. Being prequalified says little more than maybe the buyers will get the mortgage, and then again maybe they won't.

Although in many cases a prequalification letter is worth little more than the paper it's written on, it may not be totally worthless. Sometimes such a letter indicates that someone checked your financial information and ran a credit report on you. But unfortunately, that someone wasn't a lender who was willing to commit to backing you.

A Long Road Ahead: Start the Preapproval Process Early

It's wise to start the preapproval process early because it can take some time to complete. The lender has to evaluate your application, secure a credit check, and perhaps verify your employment and savings (for your down payment). Then your application must be sent to underwriting where secondary lenders (Fannie Mae or Freddie Mac for most loans) will check it over and give approval. Only then will the lender issue the preapproval letter. The process might take only a few days (if the lender does it electronically), or it might take a month or more if a problem is discovered that you must correct.

By the way, some lenders will offer you a preliminary preapproval letter. This means that they have taken your application and have completed a credit report, but they have not yet obtained underwriting approval. A preliminary preapproval letter will say that you're preapproved subject to underwriting. It's not as good as an actual preapproval letter, but it is easier to get, particularly if you're short on time.

Another good reason to start early getting your preapproval letter is that you may discover that there's a problem that will take time to resolve; for example, a credit check might show that you have unpaid bills, late payments, or even a bankruptcy. Although it's true you should already be aware of these difficulties, we're only human, and sometimes we forget or choose to forget (or we didn't share that ugly detail with our new spouse). If a problem crops up during the preapproval process, you usually have time to do something about it. If you wait until you're in the midst of a mortgage deal, the delay could cause you to lose the home you want most.

As noted in the Hazard earlier in this chapter, there may be an error at the credit bureau. Perhaps the bureau has mistaken you for someone else. Or it didn't receive word that a loan was paid off. Or a lender improperly stated that you hadn't paid when you had. In short, almost anything can go wrong, and until you check it out, you won't know. These examples give you good reason to check your own credit with the three national credit bureaus in advance of when you need it. For a nominal fee, the credit bureaus will give you a report on your credit.

1. Equifax: Telephone: 1-800-685-1111 (http://www.equifax.com)
2. Experian: 1-800-682-7654 (http://www.experian.com/product/consumer)
3. Trans Union: 1-800-916-8800 (http://www.tuc.com)

Problems other than credit sometimes crop up when you apply for a mortgage. You might not have enough income to warrant a mortgage as large as you want. Or perhaps in order to get a mortgage, you'll need to put 20 percent down instead of 10 percent. On a $125,000 home, that's an extra $12,500 you'll have to come up with in cash!

In short, the problems that can and often do arise are endless. And you won't know about them until you actually apply for the mortgage, which is one of the big reasons that sellers are so worried about buyers who don't have preapproval letters.

Directions, Please: Where to Go to Get Preapproval

Any legitimate lender can preapprove you and your spouse. And remember, it should cost you nothing except the $50 or so for the credit report. If a lender wants to charge for preapproval, walk out. There are plenty of other lenders out there. Here are your choices, most of which can be found in the yellow pages:

1. Banks offer mortgages, but they don't specialize in them. Banks spend more of their efforts on car loans and commercial finance.

2. Savings and loan associations (S&Ls) are designed primarily to offer residential mortgages. They underwent massive changes after the S&L loan debacle of the late 1970s and early 1980s, and many of those that survived were converted into banks.

3. Mortgage brokers are the new lenders of choice for most first-time home-buyers. Mortgage brokers are individuals or companies that supply the retail service for major lenders, such as banks and insurance companies. These brokers provide the storefront, so to speak, that the more traditional lenders no longer offer. A good mortgage broker will offer a wide variety of mortgage types from dozens of different lenders. It's like shopping at a grocery store for potato chips rather than tracking down a Frito-Lay company outlet. All the brands are readily available. And you won't be paying more by dealing with a mortgage broker instead of a direct lender, such as a bank. Interest rates and fees are almost always comparable.

4. Mortgage bankers are lenders of mortgages similar to a regular bank. However, whereas a regular bank offers consumer services, such as checking and savings accounts, safe-deposit boxes, commercial loans, and so forth, the mortgage banker has only one function: making real estate loans. Some of the country's largest independent lenders are mortgage bankers that deal directly with consumers.

5. Credit unions.

The Internet has become another venue for finding a lender of choice. Within the next few years, the vast majority of mortgages may originate on the Internet. The reasons for the growth of Internet mortgages are convenience and savings. Although you can get preapproved on the Internet and find some of the best financing available, you must choose your lender wisely. Some online lenders to check out include the following:

▶ E-Loan (http://www.eloan.com)
▶ Lending Tree (http://www.lendingtree.com)

Touring a lender's Web site is an enlightening experience. Almost all of the loan sites will calculate your monthly payment if you input the principal, interest rate, and term of your mortgage. Most sites also include "wizards" that will recommend the type of loan that you should get based on your financial information.

Using the Internet for preapproval is not only convenient, there are also discounts available. Internet loans are not true retail mortgages. They are somewhere between retail (from a mortgage broker) and wholesale (from a direct lender, such as a bank). There is no storefront or secretarial staff, so the savings get passed on to you. The discount can sometimes be as much as 1 percent of the loan amount or more. In addition, some Internet lenders will offer to reimburse you for the costs of both the appraisal and the credit report if you follow through and get the mortgage from them.

But be careful. Not all lenders on the Internet are for real. It's very hard to judge whether you're dealing with a true mortgage company or some guy working out of his garage. You don't want to send your intimate financial information to a fly-by-night operation that might use the information unscrupulously. If you don't recognize a lender's name as that of a legitimate company, check the lender with the Better Business Bureau and with banking officials in the lender's state. *Never send money or reveal any of your personal financial information until you know you're dealing with a legitimate lender.*

Although much can be done electronically and by fax, at some point you have to go to an office and meet with the lender or an escrow officer to present your documentation and to sign the loan agreement. Still, electronic lending is definitely the wave of the future. For more information on getting a loan over the Internet, see Appendix B.

Tollbooth 2.2 helps you determine the mortgage you may be able to afford, based on the formulas used by lenders and mortgage brokers.

▶ Saving for Your Trip: Budgeting for a Mortgage

Once you've been preapproved for a mortgage, you know how large a loan you can get. But finding a home is often a compromise between what you and your spouse *want* and what you can really *afford*. You've heard the expression, "champagne taste on a beer budget." Housing is no different: Getting preapproved only tells you how much financing you can get. Now let's take a look at deciding how much you and your spouse will feel comfortable spending. After all, you have to pay the bills.

First, look at your total monthly income and expenditures and see how much is left over for a house payment. Again, Roadmap 1.3 in Chapter 1 will help you tally your current expenses. Try to be candid: If you haven't already done this exercise, make sure that you put down what you and your spouse are *actually* spending, not what you *wish* you were spending.

Tollbooth 2.2

Calculating How Much House You Can Qualify for

Principal borrowed: $200,000.00

Annual payments: 12

Total payments: 360*

Annual interest rate: 6.00 percent

Periodic interest rate: 0.5000 percent

Regular mortgage payment amount: $1,199.10

Note: The following numbers are estimates. See an amortization schedule for more accurate values.

Total repaid: $431,676.00

Total interest paid: $231,676.00

Payment	Principal	Interest	Cum Prin	Cum Int	Prin Bal
1	$199.10	1000.00	199.10	1000.00	$199800.90
2	200.10	999.00	399.20	1999.00	199600.80
3	201.10	998.00	600.30	2997.00	199399.70
4	202.10	997.00	802.40	3994.00	199197.60
5	203.11	995.99	1005.51	4989.99	198994.49
6	204.13	994.97	1209.64	5984.96	198790.36
7	205.15	993.95	1414.79	6978.91	198585.21
8	206.17	992.93	1620.96	7971.84	198379.04
9	207.20	991.90	1828.16	8963.74	198171.84
10	208.24	990.86	2036.40	9954.60	197963.60

*only the first 10 payments of a typical 30-year mortgage are shown here.

Also, don't make the mistake of thinking that your only housing expense will be your mortgage payment. As mentioned at the beginning of the chapter, homeowners face many costs that renters do not. Use Tollbooth 2.3 to help you plan for these expenditures. Add these expenses to your previous total.

The amount left over from your income may now seem terribly small. This number is probably much smaller than the amount the lender says you can qualify for a mortgage payment. If that's the case, it's time for compromise. Ask yourself what you might be willing to give up to own your first home.

Tollbooth 2.3

Calculating Additional Monthly Expenses if You Buy a Home

Property taxes and home insurance payments (if your lender hasn't already figured these costs into your preapproval mortgage payment)	$ _____
Yard maintenance and landscaping	_____
Home repairs (buying a newer house helps here)	_____
Additional utilities (those that your landlord currently pays: gas, electric, water, garbage, sewage, and cable)	_____
Homeowners association dues	_____
Total monthly expenses less mortgage payment	_____

Remember, buying a home is not like purchasing furniture or a car, nor is it like renting. Furniture and cars decline in value the moment they leave the showroom, and paying rent is often viewed as money thrown out the window each month. In contrast, your home will likely increase in value over time. If it's worth more than it was the month before, you've got appreciation. And there are many other great advantages about home ownership to consider. Therefore, you may be willing to tighten your belt so you can pay more for a home of your own than you would be willing to spend on a rental. Think of your home purchase as an investment. On the other hand, don't go overboard and commit yourself to a payment that will sink you. Stretch yourself, but don't dream impossible dreams.

Finally, before we move on to other costs you need to consider, discuss with your spouse what's most important to each of you in choosing a home. The emotional aspect of buying a home can be extremely intense. Women generally view their homes as nests, men as their castles and investments. When you're buying a home together, talk about the kinds of compromises you're each willing to make, which can eliminate conflict when the time comes to choose.

Roadmap 2.1 helps you establish your own priorities: the housing characteristics that are essential to each of you, the features on which you will compromise if necessary, and the things that don't matter at all. Then use

Roadmap 2.1

What Matters Most to You?

Before you start house hunting, consider which factors are most important to you. Rate on a scale of 1 (unimportant) to 10 (very important):

Proximity to work	——	Storage space	——
Quality and proximity of schools	——	Room for hobby	——
Condition/age of house	——	Room for entertaining	——
Type and age of roof	——	Home office	——
Fireplace(s)	——	Ease of maintenance	——
Landscaping, view	——	Mature trees	——
Garage requirements	——	Light and sunshine	——
Number of bedrooms	——	Sidewalks	——
Number of baths	——	Lot size and usability	——
Pool or spa	——	Expandability	——
Computer wiring	——	Security system	——
Large kitchen	——	Breakfast nook	——
Deck, patio	——	Formal entry	——
Separate dining room	——	Workshop	——
Family room/great room	——	Formal living room	——
Community pool	——	Neighborhood park	——
Gate guarded	——	Ample guest parking	——
Active adult (over 55)	——	Tot lot	——
Neighborhood rules (CC&Rs*)	——	Other	——

Covenants, conditions, & restrictions

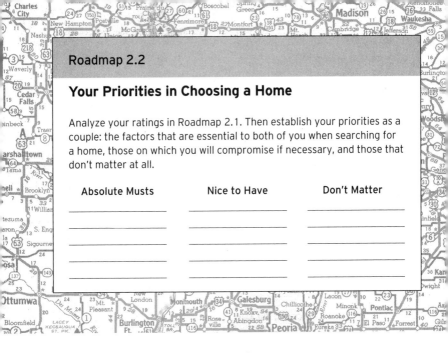

Roadmap 2.2

Your Priorities in Choosing a Home

Analyze your ratings in Roadmap 2.1. Then establish your priorities as a couple: the factors that are essential to both of you when searching for a home, those on which you will compromise if necessary, and those that don't matter at all.

Absolute Musts	Nice to Have	Don't Matter

Roadmap 2.2 to fill out the profile of your needs and wants. The answers will help you consider the housing characteristics you both want. Even though these desires may not seem like financial factors, they will affect your decision regarding the type of house you can afford to buy.

Additional Tolls: Taxes And Insurance

Sometimes when a lender preapproves a monthly mortgage payment, that figure includes property taxes as well as fire and homeowners insurance. It's called PITI in the lending trade: principal, interest (on the mortgage), taxes, and insurance.

But sometimes the preapproved monthly figure does not include taxes and insurance. If you put less than 20 percent down, the taxes and insurance are normally part of your monthly payment. If you put more than 20 percent down, taxes and insurance are paid separately if you choose. If you decide to pay taxes and insurance separately, be sure to include them as additional monthly expenses.

A useful rule of thumb for determining taxes and insurance is to calculate 2 percent of the likely value of the home if it is in a low-tax state, or 4–5 percent if it is in a high-tax state. Divide the result by 12 to find the monthly cost for taxes and insurance. (If you don't know whether the tax rate in your state is high or low, ask your real estate agent.)

Owning a home is not only about high costs. Your home can also return some money to you. All property taxes and interest on your mortgage (up to certain limits) are tax deductible. You can view the total amount of your tax savings as additional monthly income.

Calculating Your Tax Savings

Here's how to determine the approximate amount you will save on your taxes. First, ask the lender what the total interest on your mortgage will be for the first full year. Next, ask your real estate agent what the taxes will be on the property. A good realtor should be able to give you a fairly accurate guess. Now add these two figures together to generate an estimate of your total deduction.

$13,500 (interest) + 3,500 (taxes) = $17,000 (total deduction)

This large deduction will help balance out the high mortgage payments you may struggle with. Receiving a hefty deduction is the good part of paying for a mortgage. To determine how much that deduction will save you in taxes, check with your accountant to see what your marginal tax bracket is. If it happens to be 28 percent, here are your approximate savings:

$17,000 (deductible amount) × 28 percent (tax bracket) =
$4,760 (tax savings)

Caution: Remember, we're dealing with a marginal tax bracket that could change. If your income decreases, you may fall into a lower tax bracket, which would reduce your tax savings.

By making payments on your first home, you will save roughly $400 a month on federal taxes during the first year. You can then have your employer reduce your federal tax withholding by $400 a month, thus increasing your take-home pay by a similar amount. Keep in mind that we're only considering federal income taxes at this point. If you have to pay state income taxes, you should also have tax savings on them.

Remember that as time goes by, the amount of your mortgage payment that pays the interest will decrease, and the amount that goes to principal will increase (in a standard amortized mortgage). (Amortization is the removal of a financial liability via regular, fixed payments over time.) This shift will affect your tax savings for subsequent years, because interest payments are tax-deductible; principal payments are not.

When you consider your tax savings, you've suddenly got more money that you can use to pay for a mortgage. That is one of the reasons that your lender may have calculated a higher affordable payment for you than you thought reasonable.

Other Tolls: The Interest Rate Affects Your Mortgage

The size of your mortgage depends not only on the monthly payment you can qualify for, but also on interest rates. The higher the interest rate, the smaller the mortgage you can qualify for; the lower the interest rate, the larger the mortgage. Because a substantial portion of the price of the home will be covered by the mortgage, interest rates indirectly determine how much you can afford to pay for your new home.

Tollbooth 2.4 shows the amazing variance in the size of the mortgage you can qualify for depending on the interest rate. The higher the interest rate, the lower the maximum mortgage you can qualify for. This rule of thumb is the reason why it is important for you and your spouse to purchase when interest rates are low, if at all possible.

More Tolls Ahead: Property Taxes

No matter where you live in the United States, you will be taxed each year on your home. Property taxes are "ad valorem," which means they are paid according to the value of the property. The more valuable your property, the higher the taxes. The less valuable your property, the lower the taxes.

Property taxes must be paid or the state or local government, after following a defined set of legal procedures, can take the property away from you and sell it to recover the unpaid taxes. Actually, that almost never happens with improved property (property that includes a house) because your lender, as part of the mortgage agreement you signed, requires you to keep up the property taxes. If you don't pay your taxes, your lender will foreclose (cancel the loan and recover the asset used to secure the loan) to protect itself. Lenders have a service (borrowers pay for it in their closing costs) that notifies them when property taxes are unpaid and the state puts a lien on a property. (A lien is any legal claim against an asset for money that must be paid when the asset is sold.)

Tollbooth 2.4

How Big a Mortgage Your Monthly Payment Will Buy

Mortgage payment of $1,322 for a 30-year fixed mortgage

Rate	Mortgage Amount
5%	$246,000
6%	220,000
7%	200,000
8%	182,000
9%	164,000
10%	151,000

Mortgage payment of $1,322 for a 15-year fixed mortgage

Rate	Mortgage Amount
5%	$167,000
6%	157,000
7%	147,000
8%	138,000
9%	130,000
10%	123,000

Estimating Your Tolls: Your Property Taxes May Be Different from the Seller's

When anticipating how high your property taxes will be, it is important to keep in mind that the amount of taxes the seller paid on the property may be irrelevant. Your own tax bill could be significantly higher.

For example, suppose you're looking at an older home, and the seller is paying only $900 in taxes. The tax bill could be based on an assessment made years ago. In your state, property may be reassessed when it is sold. If you and your spouse purchase the house, the sale will be recorded in the assessor's office. Because the sales price is the best indication of the home's value, the assessor may reassess or redetermine your property taxes. If you complain about the reassessment, the assessor will inspect the property to determine if the sales price was fair. If it was, you must now pay taxes on the *new* value of the home, which means your taxes may be substantially higher than what the old owner was paying.

That's why checking the existing taxes on a property in a state that reassesses upon sale, as some buyers are prone to do, is a waste of time and can result in a false estimate of what your monthly payments will be. If you're not sure how your state handles property taxes, ask a good real estate agent.

▶ Paying the First Toll: How Much Down Payment Can You Afford?

The size of the mortgage you get and, correspondingly, the amount you can pay for your home depend heavily on the size of your down payment. The larger your down payment, the larger the loan you're likely to qualify for.

Unfortunately, this dynamic is a big trouble spot for most first-time borrowers. After all, your entire down payment must come from savings. You don't have another house that you can sell, so you have no equity to roll over. So how do you come up with a sufficient down payment?

It's probably not a good idea to delay your purchase until you and your spouse have saved up for a large down payment. In most markets, the longer you wait, the more expensive the houses become. Also, if interest rates are rising, you want to get into the market as soon as possible.

Unfortunately, lenders do not allow you to make the down payment from borrowed money. However, if you borrowed the money a long time ago, say six months or more, the lender usually won't consider it to have been borrowed specifically to make a home purchase, and you might get away with using the borrowed money as your down payment. But extra loan payments will affect your borrowing ability.

Frequently parents, grandparents, or other relatives will give or loan money to first-time homebuyers to help with the down payment. (Generally, gifts of up to $11,000 annually are nontaxable.) In the past, lenders frowned on these gifts and loans. They do so far less today, although they may still want to get the names of the donors on the mortgage, and they may require them to qualify for it as well.

To prevent these problems, deposit the gift into your account several months before you apply for the mortgage. Then if the lender asks where you got the money, you can say it was a gift, but you don't need to say that it was a gift specifically for buying a home.

Finally, it's important to understand that you will need cash for more than the down payment; you will also have to pay closing costs. You may also want to buy some new furniture for your house, and it's best to keep a reserve in case of emergencies. Therefore, you should hold on to your savings as much as possible. Of course, the larger your down payment, the smaller your mortgage and your monthly payments. However, keep in mind that putting down an extra percent or two won't make that much difference in your monthly payments.

Generally speaking, you won't need the full down payment until the deal closes, which usually occurs at the time you move in. It could be a couple of months or more between the time your offer is accepted by the seller and the time the deal closes. However, you'll need to show the lender that you have the money to put down by referring to a savings or similar account. And you'll need to have an earnest money deposit available immediately after the seller accepts your offer.

Few people are in the lucky position of being able to put down more money than the lender requires. Most of us strain to get the minimum down payment. If you are fortunate enough to have the option of putting more money down, should you do it? A lot depends on what your goals are. Putting more money down will reduce the amount of your mortgage and, in turn, your monthly payments. But unless you add a huge sum above the minimum amount into the down payment, your monthly payments won't be reduced by much, and you won't have that cash available if you need it for other purposes. You can, however, obtain a home equity loan (a second mortgage) if you need cash in the future.

Another way of looking at the dilemma of the size of your down payment relates to the amount of interest involved. If you have an extra $10,000 and put it in the bank, you'll be lucky to get 4 percent interest. On the other hand, if you put the money into the down payment, you'll be avoiding paying 7 or 8 percent interest on the mortgage. Therefore, you'll be saving 4 or 5 percent. Should you do it? It's really a matter of how you view money.

What this example shows is that the difference between the amount a lender says you can qualify for and the amount you will feel comfortable with may be worlds apart. If you and your spouse are good at budgeting and keeping track of your checkbook, chances are you'll find the lender's figure okay. On the other hand, if your checkbook tends to be off each month and you can never stick to a budget, then perhaps you'd best look for a lower down payment.

Which Way to Turn? Five Types of Mortgages

There is an alphabet soup of mortgages out there. Fortunately, most of these fall within a few broad categories. This section describes the most frequently used mortgages along with their major variations; namely, five categories of mortgages in terms of their benefits to you. You'll find that there is some overlap among the categories.

1. low down payment mortgages
2. low monthly payment mortgages
3. easy-qualifying mortgages
4. jumbo mortgages
5. special situation mortgages

Route #1. Low Down Payment Mortgages

Because finding the cash is usually the hardest part of most real estate purchases, let's consider mortgages that allow you to pay a minimal down payment. All of these mortgages (with one exception, as we'll see) involve having some sort of insurance or guarantee of your performance. That's why you can get away with putting less down.

FHA Mortgages. The Federal Housing Administration (FHA) insures these mortgages. From the first-time buyer's perspective, they are desirable because the standard down payment is only 5 percent. (In some rural areas and within some special programs, that figure can go as low as 3 percent.) This means that if the house you're purchasing costs $100,000, you only have to come up with $5,000 as a down payment! However, there are restrictions and other negative aspects of this type of mortgage.

FHA loans are available from banks, savings and loans (S&Ls), and mortgage brokers. Just ask about these loans and almost anyone in the lending field can explain how they operate, and if they are a viable option for you and your spouse.

VA (Veterans Administration) Mortgages. The Department of Veterans Affairs in Washington, D.C., guarantees these mortgages (as opposed to FHA insured loans). They are available only to veterans of the U.S. Armed Forces who served for a specific number of days during certain periods of time. You must check with the VA to see what these dates are, as they are occasionally changed, and to obtain a certificate of eligibility.

If you or your spouse is a qualified veteran, a VA mortgage can be an excellent loan for you because no down payment is required, although you may have to pay something if the house costs more than the maximum mortgage amount allowed. If the home costs $90,000, your down payment is zero! If you are a retired vet and want more information on this type of mortgage, see Appendix B for other books on this topic.

Insured Conventional Mortgages. These loans are the standard conventional mortgages. They are 80 percent of either the appraised value of the home or the selling price, whichever is lower. However, lenders can increase the amount borrowed to 90 percent, or even 95 percent in some cases, provided you are an excellent credit risk and there is private mortgage insurance (PMI) on the loan.

PMI comes from private companies and covers the first 20 percent of the mortgage. In other words, if the buyer defaults on the loan (that means you), and the lender takes back the property and is unable to sell it for the mortgage amount, PMI will cover up to the first 20 percent of the lender's loss. In most cases, this is the entire loss incurred by the lender.

Most private lenders offer PMI mortgages. But you will have to have a sterling credit rating and a strong income to qualify. In addition, the property must be in a choice area with strong resale potential. Therefore, PMI is not for everyone. But for some first-time buyers, it can be a wonderful way to get a mortgage with a small down payment.

Seller Financing. This type of loan is the oldest method of getting a small down payment. In addition to acquiring a new mortgage from an institutional lender, you get a second mortgage from the seller. For example, you get an 80 percent loan from the bank and the seller lends you an additional 15 percent. You now can get the property for as little as 5 percent down, plus closing costs! And you don't have to be qualified for the second mortgage because it's coming from the seller.

The problem with this type of loan is that sellers usually do not want to give mortgages because of the risk involved (you may not be able to repay them) and because they need the cash to buy another property. Thus, while you may find a seller who will "carry back" some "paper" (as these loans are referred to in the trade), it is not likely to happen.

In addition, many institutional lenders today will set not only a maximum loan amount, but also a maximum combined loan amount. This means that you may get 80 percent of the price from the lender, but the same lender will not allow you to borrow more than 10 percent from the seller for a combined total of 90 percent.

Conforming Loans. Conforming loans adhere to the underwriting standards of Fannie Mae and Freddie Mac, the "secondary lenders" that lend money to the institution that lends to you. Both Fannie Mae and Freddie Mac have a wide variety of low down payment mortgages. Indeed, Fannie Mae has experimented with no down payment mortgages! Ask a mortgage broker for information on their various programs. You may also want to check out their Web sites, which are loaded with information on their various programs: www.fanniemae.com and www.freddiemac.com.

Route #2. Low Monthly Payment Mortgages

So far, we have examined mortgage types that help first-time buyers purchase a home with a lower down payment. Now let's consider mortgages that are specifically designed to give you lower monthly payments. (Note that some low monthly payment mortgages can be combined with low down payment mortgages. For example, you can combine an adjustable-rate mortgage with a PMI mortgage.)

Adjustable-Rate Mortgage (ARM). An adjustable-rate mortgage can cut your mortgage payment by a third or more, at least in the early days of the mortgage. For example, if your payment is going to be $900 a month with a fixed-rate mortgage, an adjustable-rate mortgage can initially cut that down to $600 a month or even less.

This adjustability has two important ramifications, especially for first-time buyers. First, with a lower monthly payment, you and your spouse may be able to get into a house and a neighborhood that you would not otherwise qualify for. Second, because you're making a lower monthly payment, it will be easier for you to maintain a higher quality lifestyle.

On the other hand, ARMs have some significant drawbacks. The most important disadvantage is that the low monthly payments could last a relatively short time (months or, at the outside, a few years). After that, the monthly payment could rise quickly to a point at which it's higher than if you had initially opted for a fixed-rate mortgage. But remember you were hundreds of dollars ahead each month during the initial period of the loan. Therefore, it may take a few years of higher interest rates to make taking out the ARM a bad idea. The following sections describe some of the key benefits and features of an ARM.

An ARM is particularly useful if you and your spouse are planning on living in the home for only a short period of time, let's say three years or less. During that time, you could save a considerable amount on monthly payments compared to a fixed-rate mortgage if you plan to stay in your home for several more years.

The ARM is also useful during periods of temporarily high interest rates. The ARM allows you to get into a property at a lower than market rate when market rates are high. Then, when rates have fallen several years later, you can refinance to a lower rate mortgage. ARMs are complex mortgages, but they can be a real boon to first-time buyers, and you and your spouse should seriously consider them as long as you take into account their drawbacks. For more information on ARMs, see the Appendix.

Graduated Payment Mortgage (GPM). A graduated payment mortgage is designed specifically for first-time homebuyers. It has a low initial interest rate that increases by incremental steps at designated periods of time (usually every year or so). Each step raises the monthly payments by predetermined amounts. Eventually, perhaps seven years down the road, the interest rate is higher than the market rate when you made your purchase.

The idea behind the GPM is that as you get older and, presumably, as your income grows, so too will the mortgage payment. You will have low payments when you first start out, and then later, as you're more able to pay, you'll pay more. Unlike an ARM, in which the mortgage *adjusts* according to an index and the amount of future payments is unknown, the GPM is a *fixed* interest rate mortgage with a rate that changes at predetermined times and in predetermined amounts.

If you and your spouse see yourselves on a career course that will provide you with increasing income, the GPM could be a good mortgage for you. The problem, of course, is that the payment schedule is inflexible, and if your careers nosedive, you might not be able to make the increasingly higher monthly payments. You could lose your house.

On the good side, however, you never have to worry about negative amortization with a GPM. And you won't get any shocks. You'll know well in advance what every monthly payment will be. GPMs are often combined with FHA mortgages. Ask your lender for more information about them in your area.

Short-Term Mortgages. Short-term mortgages are often recommended to first-time buyers. It combines the best features of the adjustable-rate mortgage and the fixed-rate mortgage.

Here's how it works. The short-term mortgage has two different time periods: an *initial* loan period and then a *secondary* loan period. Although the terms can vary greatly, during the initial time period you generally have a lower than market, fixed-rate mortgage. During the secondary time period, you have a rather ugly adjustable-rate mortgage.

For example, the current market rate may be 8 percent. Let's say you get a three-year mortgage. During the first three years of your mortgage, your payments may be based on a 7 percent interest rate amortized (paid in equal payments) over 30 years, just as if you had a true 30-year, fixed-rate mortgage. You save 1 percent for the three years.

At the end of year three, however, the mortgage either comes due as a balloon (a large single payment) or converts to an adjustable-rate mortgage with a high margin and a volatile index. At this point, you would usually end up paying more than market rate interest. That's when you and your spouse should refinance or sell.

Short-term mortgages as described above are available in a variety of terms, the most common being three, five, seven, and 10 years, all amortized over a 30-year period. A mortgage is sometimes called by its term and its period of time; for example, "a 3/30 mortgage" or a "7/30." The shorter the initial fixed interest rate period, the lower the initial interest rate.

The advantage here is that you and your spouse would know in advance what your monthly payment would be for a fixed period of time. If you're like most people, you would probably plan to sell before that time period ends, and hence, you would get the benefits without incurring the drawback of the high adjustable interest rate.

There are a number of variations of the short-term mortgage, the most common being a convertible mortgage that starts out as a rather pleasant adjustable-rate mortage with a good index, reasonable margins, and fair steps. However, at a certain point, usually between years three and five, you have the one-time option of converting it to a fixed-rate mortgage at current interest rates.

Interest-Only Loans. One of the more recent entries in the home mortgage field and another possibility for first-time homebuyers is the interest-only loan. This is a fixed-rate mortgage. As its name implies, instead of paying back interest plus principal each month, you pay back only interest. However, because of the mathematics of amortization (payback) of loans, this is only a small monthly savings, perhaps in the neighborhood of less than 5 percent of the monthly payment. (Most of the interest is paid at the beginning of a mortgage, most of the principal at the end.) If you and your spouse are not planning to keep the property long and want a slightly lower fixed-interest-rate mortgage, this is an option you might consider.

Balloon-Payment Mortgage. A balloon-payment mortgage will sometimes earn a first-time buyer a lower interest rate and, therefore, a lower monthly payment. But beware: You could end up losing your house if you don't take timely action. A balloon mortgage is any type of mortgage that is not fully amortized, which means it is not paid off in equal payments. Homeowners usually carry such a loan for a fairly short time (five years or so), during which they make payments only on the interest. At the end of a specified period of time, the mortgage is all due in one huge (balloon) payment.

Route #3. Easy-Qualifying Mortgages

So far, the types of mortgages that have been described allow you to buy a home with less money down or with a lower monthly payment. However, sometimes the most difficult issue is not payments or cash but your credit. Sometimes because of a bad credit history or because you don't have a strong income, you cannot qualify for the types of mortgages we've been describing. Again, this problem is frequently the case for first-time borrowers, who are often in the process of establishing their credit and growing their careers. There are several specific options available to you.

Seller Financing. Obtaining financing from the seller was briefly described earlier, but it bears extra consideration for first-time buyers who have trouble qualifying for a mortgage. When a seller gives you part of a home's purchase price (whether a house, condo, townhouse, or co-op) in the form of a mortgage, there's usually little or no need to qualify. You may have to submit a credit report to the seller, but usually that's all you need to do. Compare that process to the extensive documentation, the minimum income requirement, and good credit demanded by an institutional lender. You'll quickly see that getting a loan from the seller is a great way to get easy financing.

The trick is to find a seller who's willing and able to give you financing. A fair number of sellers will help out by taking back a second mortgage, but usually not for more than 10 percent of the sales price. Remember, they usually need the cash to buy another house themselves, and often they owe a lot on their own mortgage.

So if you and your spouse are first-time buyers with a problem qualifying for a new mortgage, it's a good idea to spend some time going through a broker's listings looking for sellers who either have their property paid off or have only a small mortgage on it. If they own their property, they might give you a mortgage for 80 percent or more of the price. Or they may give you a 20 or 30 percent mortgage, and you could get an institutional first mortgage for 50 or 60 percent, which is much easier to qualify for.

Why would a seller agree to help you with financing? Sometimes sellers don't want cash; they want income. And mortgage interest is usually among the highest long-term interest available. A retired couple might see you as the perfect solution to their problem! Still, this solution is a long shot. You won't find many sellers who both have a lot of cash in their property and are willing to help finance. But they do exist. Just remember that you won't be able to be as picky in selecting the neighborhood or the house.

Assumable Mortgages. Another way to avoid qualifying difficulties is to find a house that already has a big assumable mortgage on it. The term *assumable* means that you can take over the mortgage. Most mortgages are currently not assumable. In other words, when the current owners sell the home, they must pay off the mortgage, and the new buyer can't take it on. But a few mortgages are assumable. Talk to your broker about homes available with assumable mortgages.

Route #4. Jumbo Mortgages

Jumbo mortgages are very big mortgages that are frequently found in high-cost areas. The amount at which a mortgage becomes a "jumbo" changes frequently, so check with a lender. If you and your spouse live in an area where housing prices are very high, you may have no choice but to take a jumbo mortgage, which carries slightly higher interest rates (depending on the qualifications of the buyer). For that reason, lenders love them.

If you need a jumbo mortgage, check with a bank or S&L in your area, although some mortgage brokers handle them, too. Loan programs vary enormously and sometimes can be set up to specifically meet your needs. These are really custom loans tailored for specific needs and properties.

Route #5. Special Situation Mortgages

There are a number of other mortgage types that are used for special situations, none of which are really recommended for first-time buyers. Nevertheless, you may be introduced to them by an agent or seller, so you will want to know something about them.

Lease/Option. If you and your spouse are first-time buyers who have little to no money for a down payment, you may want to consider a lease/option. It's a pay-as-you-rent way to save money for a down payment. Be aware, however, that it requires a great deal of discipline to make it work.

There is no mortgage involved in a lease/option agreement. Instead, you and the seller agree on an option-to-purchase plan, which is detailed in a signed agreement. According to the plan, you agree to rent the seller's property for a number of years (usually one to three years). During that time, the payments you make will be divided into two parts. One part will represent rent, the other will represent option money that will go toward a down payment. When you have paid enough money each month to equal a full down payment, you will then obtain a mortgage, and the seller will give you a deed to the property.

For example, suppose you and your spouse find a condo you like. It costs $90,000, and you need a minimum of $9,000 as a down payment. But you have no money at all to put down. So you arrange for a lease/option. Your payment might be $900 a month; $525 of that might go toward rent and $375 toward the down payment. After 24 months, you will have paid the seller $9,000 ($375 × 24) plus rent. At that time, you would exercise the option to purchase and obtain a 90 percent mortgage. The seller would credit you with a $9,000 down payment, and you would buy the property.

A lease/option can be a good deal for first-time borrowers because it effectively forces you to save the down payment. And usually the amount you pay toward rent is less than market price. For example, the condo might have a market rental value of $700 a month, but the seller reduces that to $525 to get a future sale. You, on the other hand, pay an extra couple of hundred dollars above the fair rental value each month because you know that money is going toward a future down payment.

What you have to be sure of in a lease/option is that you can qualify for a new first mortgage when the option time is up. If you pay for the two years as outlined in the above example, and then discover you can't qualify for a mortgage, you won't be able to complete the purchase. In that case, you'll lose the extra money you've put into the property.

Although many sellers honestly hope you'll ultimately be able to buy their home, some sophisticated investors play the lease/option "game." They particularly seek out first-time buyers who don't have a prayer of qualifying for a new mortgage. These unscrupulous sellers are counting on their buyers being unable to qualify for a mortgage and unable to exercise the option. They do it to rake in a couple of hundred extra dollars a month in rent!

You will find many sellers willing to sell on a lease/option when the real estate market is down. They can't sell for a cash deal, so they take the next best thing. In a healthy market, however, you are not likely to find many legitimate sellers offering lease/options.

If you decide to go ahead with a lease/option, it's a good idea to have the deal recorded in a written agreement. That way you are assured that the seller won't sell the property to someone else while you're renting and waiting to exercise your option. Be sure to have the owner's signature notarized so the document can be recorded.

Buydowns. You may run into a buydown if you and your spouse are first-time buyers purchasing a home from a builder. To induce buyers, especially first-time buyers, to purchase new homes, builders may offer below-market interest rates on financing.

For example, the current interest rate may be 9 percent, but builders, only through their lenders, may offer 8 percent. Or the builders' lenders may offer a sliding scale; for example, 6 percent the first year, 7 percent the second year, 8 percent the third year, and, finally, the market rate of 9 percent during the fourth year. To follow this plan, builders pay the lender the difference between the market rate and the interest rate you are paying. Because builders pay the difference up front all at once, their obligation is less than the amount you would pay if you were to pay the difference yourself in monthly payments. But it still usually amounts to thousands of dollars.

Is a buydown a good deal for you and your spouse? Yes, providing the builders haven't inflated the price of the home to compensate for the better financing! If you can afford the current interest rate, you may want to ask the builders to credit you with the money it would have cost them for the buydown. For example, if the buydown were to cost them $5,000, they may be willing to take this amount off the price of the home or they may offer it to you as a credit toward the down payment if your lender will allow this.

▶ Which Road to Take? Condo, Co-Op, Townhome, or House?

Now you know something about the various types of mortgages. If you don't think you and your spouse can afford to buy a house, or if you don't think you need all that room, then you might consider buying a condominium, a co-operative, or a townhome (also called a townhouse). These are all excellent choices for first-time homebuyers just starting out. They're sound investments, comfortable, affordable, full of amenities, and they're great stepping stones to larger properties that you should be able to afford later on down the road.

Before we go any further, let's settle on a few basic definitions, courtesy of *Barron's Real Estate Handbook:*

- ▶ A condominium or condo is a system of ownership of individual units in a multiunit structure combined with joint ownership of commonly used property, such as sidewalks, hallways, and stairs.
- ▶ A cooperative or co-op is housing in which each tenant is a shareholder in the corporation that owns a building.
- ▶ A townhome is a dwelling, usually with two or more floors, attached to other similar units by common walls called "party walls."

What are the differences among these choices? Condos and co-ops are quite different. When purchasing a condo, you're truly buying real estate. It's solid property that you can touch, such as walls, floors, and ceilings, but you do not purchase the land.

When you buy a co-op, you're not buying land or property; you're buying shares in a company as if you were buying shares of GE, Ford, Microsoft, or shares of a mutual fund. You may live on the property, but you don't really own the specific roof over your head, the dirt beneath your floor, or the space around you. Taxes are paid by the property owner (the corporation), although this expense is passed on as part of your monthly maintenance. Of course, this amount is tax deductible. As a corporation, a co-op has a board of directors who have the power to approve or reject potential investors according to each individual's or family's income level or personal character. The board, however, cannot make decisions that violate the nation's civil rights laws.

Townhomes and condos have much in common; in fact, in many cases townhomes are designated as condominiums by law. Owners of townhomes usually, though not always, own the land on which their property rests. Also, most townhomes are two-story structures.

Many real estate experts predict that the comparatively low price of condos will continue to attract buyers for some time. Clearly, ease of entry into the market and appreciation of that investment are primary factors in the rising popularity of condos.

Sharing the Driving: Joint Ownership of Your Home

When you buy a house with another person, the wording of the deed determines your respective shares of ownership, your legal rights, and the disposition of the property upon the death of one of you. Depending on state law, types of joint ownership include the following:

▶ *Tenancy in common.* Each owner has the right to leave his or her share to chosen heirs.
▶ *Joint tenancy with right of survivorship.* The survivor automatically becomes complete owner.
▶ *Tenancy by the entirety.* This is a special form of joint tenancy for married couples.

If the owners have unequal shares, tenancy in common is the usual form. Except in the case of tenancy by the entirety, each owner has the right to force a division (partition) or sale of the property. Therefore, because you're buying a home with your spouse, it's important to check with an attorney or the title company to make sure that the deed clearly states the form of ownership you and your spouse want.

Looking around the Bend: Other Factors to Consider

Wherever you live, the essential rule in homebuying is location. If you're buying a first home, start small with the lowest priced home in the best neighborhood. Then work to fix up and maintain your home so it keeps pace with other properties in the neighborhood. Check out the school districts. Good schools make a difference when you sell.

If you're thinking about a condominium or townhouse, check the quality of the construction carefully, especially the soundproofing. Talk to the other condo residents to make sure that most units are owner-occupied, and review the financial status of the complex to make certain the homeowners association is doing its job to maintain the property and control expenses.

Travel Light: Be Optimistic!

There is every reason in the world to keep a positive attitude when buying a house. Just don't be overanxious. Many couples typically worry about the following:

▶ *"What if we hire the wrong real estate agent?"* Everybody thinks they've hired the wrong agent, even if it's their own mother. With the exception of your mom, however, if you've hired the wrong agent, you can fire that agent and find someone else. It happens all the time.

▶ *"What if we get the wrong mortgage?"* Mortgages today are fairly easy to change, if you haven't already signed the paperwork. In the old days, your options were a 30-year, fixed-rate mortgage from a bank with a blue sign out front or a 30-year, fixed-rate mortgage from a bank with a red sign out front. In contrast, you can now almost write your own package. If you want something different, check around.

▶ *"What if we end up hating the house?"* First of all, you won't end up "hating" the house, but once you move in you are going to find things you don't like. You will find surprises. Everybody does. Remember, you can own it for a few years, make improvements or additions, change the interior, or even sell up. However, by working through Roadmaps 2.1 and 2.2 you can likely avoid making a wrong choice for the two of you.

▶ *"What if we pay too much?"* If it turns out to be the worst decision you ever made, you can always sell the house, and chalk the loss up to experience. It is difficult to forecast everything than will happen in a real estate market; what can seem like "too much" for five years after purchase can seem like a smart buy ten years down the line, when a new highway or nearby corporate headquarters arrives.

The homebuying process is rarely traumatic as long as you hold on to four fundamental concepts:

1. *Trust the process.* Yes, there will be bumps and curves, but basically the entire multitrillion dollar real estate process has been built for the sole purpose of helping you find and buy the best home that you can afford. The vast majority of real estate professionals are honest, hardworking people who are no different from you. They don't want to cheat you.

They want you to be successful because that's how they get paid. There are liars and thieves in all businesses. You can avoid them by asking the right questions. Again, trust the process.

2. *Keep a quality professional on your side every step of the way.* Search for a real estate agent you can trust, and you'll be able to work together on this transaction and on others in the future.

3. *The more you know about a house before you buy it, the better off you're going to be.* There is nothing more important in a real estate purchase than the seller's honest disclosure of the problems with his property. Odds are you're not going to get that honest disclosure, but there are ways around that, too, via the inspection process.

4. *Learn as much about the neighborhood as you can before you sign anything.* Find out about previous use—was it a landfill?—any previous flooding in the area, etc.

You are about to see that great homebuying success is available to you. All you have to do is step up and say, "Okay, let's do it!"

Learn the Language

Key Terms to Know When Buying a Home

Adjustable-rate mortgage (ARM) A mortgage with payments that increase or decrease based on changes in the economy.

Amortization The process of paying off a debt by predetermined periodic payments, including principal and interest.

Balloon payment The payment of the mortgage principal that is due at a predetermined time, and that may also contain payment of accrued interest.

Convertible ARM An adjustable-rate mortgage that contains a clause enabling the homeowner to fix the interest rate for the remainder of the loan during a certain open period (usually between months 13 and 60 of the loan term).

Credit scoring Assigning a numerical value to various financial factors in the borrower's total credit picture to determine the risk of lending to that borrower.

Debt ratios The comparison of a buyer's housing costs to his or her gross or net effective income, based on the loan program used (housing ratio); the comparison of a buyer's total long-term debt to his or her gross or net effective income, based on the loan program used (total debt ratio). (See individual programs to determine applicable ratios.)

Earnest money A good faith deposit (the down payment) given by a buyer to a seller; it is usually held in escrow until the closing.

Equity The difference between what is owed and what the property could be sold for.

Escrow An impartial holding of documents pertinent to the sale and transfer of real estate; also used to describe the long-term holding of documents (long-term escrow or escrow collection), which occurs in seller financing.

Fannie Mae Foundation A nonprofit foundation affiliated with the Federal National Mortgage Association (FNMA), designed to educate consumers about home affordability and homebuying options.

FHLMC Federal Home Loan Mortgage Corporation, also known as Freddie Mac, a part of the secondary mortage market that is particularly used to purchase loans from savings-and-loan lenders within the Federal Home Loan Bank Board.

FHA Federal Housing Administration, part of the federal government's Department of Housing and Urban Development. It exists to underwrite insured loans made by lenders to provide economical housing for moderate-income persons.

FNMA Federal National Mortgage Association, also known as Fannie Mae, a privately owned part of the secondary mortgage market used to recycle mortgages made in the primary market. The FNMA purchases conventional, FHA, and VA loans.

FRM Fixed-rate mortgage, a conventional loan with a single interest rate for the life of the loan.

FICO The Fair, Isaac & Company credit-scoring system used by many lenders to determine a borrower's ability to repay a mortgage; uses a scoring range of 300 to 850, in which the lowest score indicates highest risk.

GNMA Government National Mortgage Association, also known as Ginnie Mae, the governmental part of the secondary mortgage market that deals primarily in recycling Veterans Administration and FHA mortgages, particularly those that are highly leveraged (with a low or no down payment).

Private mortgage insurance (PMI) A type of insurance that allows people to purchase a home with a smaller-than-usual down payment. In return for the smaller down payment, the borrower pays a premium (included in the monthly mortgage).

PITI An acronym that is used to refer to the principal, interest, taxes (on property), and insurance of a home purchase.

Points A point is equal to 1 percent of the mortgage amount financed. Points are used to increase the lender's yield on the loan, which bridges the gap between the income the lender gets from conventional monies and what the lender gets from the lower rates of the VA and the FHA mortgages.

Seller financing The seller enables the borrower to finance the property, using a portion of the seller's equity in the property.

The Ultimate Air Bag

Insurance to Protect Your Spouse and Family

Regardless of the vows you and your spouse have made or are about to make, getting married implies a commitment to take care of each other. In fact, the traditional exchange of wedding cake between a bride and groom was not originally intended to smash frosting all over each spouse's face; it was meant to symbolize that the couple would feed and nourish each other.

Getting the right insurance is one way to care for each other, to make sure you're both protected if something happens to one or both of you. Even if you're living on a limited budget, you need certain kinds of insurance to protect yourselves and your assets. Insurance is a key component of financial planning. Yet despite all the motivated insurance agents out there, most Americans are underinsured.

When you spend money on insurance, you might feel like you're wasting hard-earned cash on something that produces no tangible benefit. In fact, you may go for years without collecting a dime from your insurance company. However, the opposite could also be true. You could have an accident or get sick soon after your insurance coverage starts. At that point, the benefits of insurance become real.

The subject of insurance is difficult to understand; as a result, many people pay for more insurance coverage than they need. The insurance industry is notorious for using jargon and complex presentations that baffle most people. What you don't know about insurance can hurt you in two ways:

1. You may pay too much for a policy that you could have bought more cheaply if you had understood how to compare insurers and policies.
2. The coverage you purchase may be too much or too little for your needs, or it may duplicate existing coverage in some areas and leave you unprotected in others. If you have a large claim that is not covered, you could be ruined financially.

This chapter will help you cut through the complexities of insurance so you can buy the most coverage for the fewest dollars possible. Learning about insurance is not as stimulating as uncovering the intricacies of the stock market or mutual funds, but it is equally important to your total financial plan.

There are five basic types of insurance: health, life, disability, homeowners (or renters), and car insurance. This chapter focuses on the first four because they are the most important to consider when you get married. (A car insurance policy covers your car rather than a particular person; therefore, your spouse, your entire family, and anyone you allow to drive your car on a rare exception are protected by the policy.) Let's hit the road and see what you need to know about each of the other types of insurance.

▶ Prepare for a Long Journey: Get the Right Life Insurance

For many people, life insurance is probably the most unpleasant type of insurance to discuss. As is true of other insurance policies, when you buy life insurance, you confront arcane language, complex charts and tables, and pushy salespeople. However, pure life insurance offers one difference: The insured is not the primary beneficiary of the policy. Life insurance is designed to protect the survivors of the insured. This is not to say that a life insurance policy yields no advantages while the insured is alive. Nevertheless, the main reason to purchase a policy is for the survivor benefit, which you hope that your dependents will not need to collect for a long time.

If your family or other people depend on your income, you need life insurance to help them live without your support if you pass away. The insurance contract requires that the insurance company pay your beneficiaries a set amount, called the survivor benefit, if you should die for almost any reason. (Suicide is usually excluded for the first two to three years of a policy.) Your beneficiaries can receive the money in one lump sum, free of federal income taxes. The funds should be enough to replace your paycheck, cover daily living expenses, and pay your final medical bills and burial costs. In addition, the insurance proceeds should provide income for the long-term needs of your spouse and family, such as retirement, estate taxes, and college costs.

Estimating the Toll: How Much Is Enough?

The key question in buying life insurance is figuring out how much coverage your beneficiaries really need. You should determine this amount before you listen to insurance agents' sometimes confusing sales pitches and the details of different policies. Unfortunately, assessing how much is enough is not a simple process because each family is different. As newlyweds your need for life insurance may be minimal depending on the salaries of each partner and the lifestyle you've chosen. Should you decide to have children, your need for insurance will mount, and if, for example, this is your second marriage and one or both of you has children, you will require more coverage. If you have several children, you will require more insurance than if you had just one; if one of you does not work outside the home, you will require more insurance than if both spouses earned salaries.

No formula exists, though there are two general guidelines for determining the amount of life insurance you need: (1) buy seven to 10 times your annual income and (2) buy more death benefit if you have dependents.

However, if your family has two incomes, has a thrifty lifestyle, and saves regularly, you may need less. Your estate plans and personal objectives may also warrant rethinking the amount of life insurance you carry. For instance, if you have no children but wish to leave a charitable legacy, you can easily and effectively do so by purchasing a life insurance policy and naming the charities or organizations as your beneficiaries. Do you have a large estate? You may wish to purchase a life insurance policy to pay estate taxes upon your death so that your heirs receive their full inheritance. Instead of accepting a general guideline, it makes sense to do a needs analysis of your specific situation.

Perhaps you know people who missed out on going to college, who had to move out of their family home, or who had to go back to work when their children were small or after they retired—all because the family breadwinner died without enough life insurance. Difficult life situations such as these are the first and foremost reason to buy life insurance. Insurance cannot replace you when you die, but it can replace the income you would have provided for your family. Your financial advisor can help you estimate how much insurance you need for this purpose. In most cases, you'll want the insurance amount to be enough to

▶ replace the income your family needs
▶ complete your plan for funding your children's college education
▶ pay any expenses that result from your death (probate costs, medical expenses of the final illness, funeral expenses, and estate or inheritance taxes)
▶ pay off any outstanding debts (mortgage or car loan)

Even if you aren't the family breadwinner, you should think about life insurance. For example, if you are the parent who stays home to care for your children while your spouse works at the office, your death places a significant financial burden on your surviving spouse. Your spouse will have the additional expense of child care in order to continue working, or he or she will have to quit working to stay home with the children. In either case, life insurance could provide needed funds.

The Internet offers many resources to help you calculate the insurance you need. Although these sites offer helpful calculation tools, they still may not tell you what's the right amount of insurance for you because they are based on general guidelines. When evaluating how much life insurance to purchase, you should consider your current age and health, debt load, the educational needs of your children (if you have them or plan on having them) or grandchildren (if you think you'll want to help them out, too), your total assets, and the ages of your spouse and children.

A "Virtual" Couple Finds Out How Much Life Insurance They Need

Here's a real-life needs analysis that was developed using a professional software program. John and Jill Sample, both 31, have been married two years and expect a baby in three months. Both are employed, but Jill plans to become a stay-at-home mother when the baby is born. John's income is $80,000, enough for them to live comfortably, and Jill's is $32,000, which will stop when the baby is born. They just purchased a $250,000 home with a $50,000 down payment and a $200,000 mortgage. They have $5,000 in credit card debt. They have $10,000 in mutual fund investments and $4,000 in emergency money. (They are rebuilding the latter fund to $50,000.) John's 401(k) plan is worth $15,000, and Jill's is worth $7,500. John already has life insurance provided by his employer for twice his salary, or $160,000. Jill also has employer-provided life insurance for $50,000, which will terminate when she leaves the company.

If John dies suddenly, Jill would need enough life insurance coverage to eliminate all of their debts, provide living expenses while she raises their child, pay for the child's education, and help provide for her living expenses through retirement. For the purposes of this example, let's assume $25,000 for John's funeral and final medical expenses, plus $2,500 in probate and administration costs. Let's also estimate that $50,000 needs to be invested at the time of John's death in a separate account to fund the entire college education for the child. Jill will also need $50,000 in the emergency fund.

If John were to die today (or in the next three years), he would need slightly more than $1 million in capital to pay for his immediate expenses, fund his baby's education completely, and provide for his family's living expenses. This calculation assumes that Jill does not earn an income again. After subtracting their available capital, Social Security Survivor Benefits, and existing life insurance benefits from his work-related policy, John still needs an additional $822,004 in life insurance to meet his $1,007,259 capital need.

Therefore, John would be wise to purchase at least $800,000 in 20-year term life insurance. The 20-year term is a good choice because his insurance needs will reduce drastically once his child is out (or nearly out) of college.

Consider another scenario: If Jill were to die suddenly, John might have to quit his job or provide full-time care for their child. Let's assume he would keep working and pay for child care (at least $1,500 a month). He also needs to have at least $50,000 in an emergency fund. In this case Jill would need at least $100,000 in 20-year term life insurance to pay for her child's college education and fund their emergency reserves. The cost of child care will easily add another $100,000 in the need for survivor benefits. So really Jill needs $200,000.

A Fork in the Road: Types of Life Insurance

There are two general categories of life insurance (based on the time frame of the policy) that can appropriately provide income replacement for your family: term insurance and permanent insurance. There are also two types of permanent insurance: universal and whole. Here are the basic differences, in terms of the benefits each offers. Each type has its advantages and one size doesn't fit all.

- ▶ term (provides survivor benefits only)
- ▶ permanent (provides survivor benefits only)
- ▶ universal (provides survivor and living benefits)
- ▶ whole (provides survivor and living benefits)

Term Insurance. Life insurance is most often purchased to offset the impact of premature or untimely death. Term life pays a survivor benefit, the insurance policy's "face" value, which is paid if the insured dies within a certain time period or term (for example, 10 years). If the insured lives longer than the term set by the policy, a survivor benefit is not paid. The amount of a term policy's premium is based on the life expectancy of the insured and the costs incurred by the insurance company (including a commission to the selling agent, if it is a no-load policy). (Load refers to the sales cost added to the cost of the policy itself.) Typically, the premiums you pay for term insurance increase annually, although some companies now sell term insurance with premiums that remain level for 10 or 20 years. Term insurance is useful when the need for insurance is for a specific and limited term.

For example, you only need to protect your children's college funding plans until the youngest of your children is about 22 years old. If you live longer than that, this need for insurance will disappear. Likewise, your mortgage will be paid off at some point and your need to pay for child care ceases to exist.

Permanent Insurance. Permanent insurance pays your family the face amount no matter when your death occurs. Typically, the premiums you pay for permanent insurance stay the same for your entire life. These premiums are higher in the early years than term insurance premiums, but in the later years, permanent insurance is substantially less costly.

Permanent insurance policies also build up something known as a "cash value." Your premiums are invested by the life insurance company and earn interest. You can access this cash value in an emergency by taking a loan against the insurance policy or, in some cases, by withdrawing amounts from the policy. Of course, if you borrow or spend down the cash value, the face amount will be less in the event of your death.

Permanent insurance can be either fixed or variable. If it is fixed, the underlying investments are chosen by the insurance company and the growth of your cash value is guaranteed at some stated interest rate. If the insurance is variable, the underlying investments are subaccounts that are similar to mutual fund accounts. You choose which subaccounts to invest in, and your cash value fluctuates up and down with the value of the investments in the chosen subaccounts.

Permanent insurance is best used for those insurance needs that never go away. For example, permanent insurance should be used as funding to support your spouse through a lifetime.

Different Roads for Different Reasons: Comparing Types of Life Insurance

Now that you know a little more about the two basic categories of life insurance, let's kick the tires of each type. To understand the differences better, think in terms of renting an apartment, buying a condo, or purchasing a home.

Term Insurance. Term insurance is like renting: As long as you pay your rent, you have a place to live. You usually have the choice of renting month-to-month or signing a short- or a long-term lease. At the end of the first year or lease period, the rent usually increases. And, no matter how many years you pay rent, you don't build equity.

Like renting, term life insurance is less costly to get into, but the monthly premiums go up as you age. Term policies are available for differing lengths of time, but they expire either at the end of the coverage period or when you stop paying premiums. A term policy pays out if you die during the coverage period, but it's worth nothing (other than peace of mind) if you don't.

Universal Insurance. Universal life is like purchasing a condo or townhouse; generally, the cost is higher than renting but less than purchasing a single-family home. And, as when you buy a condo, some monthly costs, such as association fees, go up, and they continue even when the mortgage is paid off. But you are building equity, and if you decide to sell, you likely will have accumulated cash and profit. Just as with buying a condo, universal life insurance costs more to get into and includes some additional fees, but you build up equity in your insurance policy. The policy then has permanent value, even if you do not die during the coverage period.

Whole Life Insurance. Whole life is like purchasing a single-family house: The cost is usually greater than the condo, you'll probably need a larger down payment, and the monthly payments will be higher. However, over the long term, the accumulated equity in your house can be substantial. In addition, you may decide to pay off the mortgage so that you won't have house payments during your retirement years.

With whole life insurance, you pay more in premiums for your survivor benefit coverage; however, you also have an opportunity to accumulate equity value over the life of the policy. Whole life insurance combines the pure insurance aspect of term insurance with a savings account. It also requires a higher premium than term, but the coverage is effective for your entire life. Its primary difference from term life is that it guarantees a survivor benefit payment as long as the policy is in force and the premiums are paid. That's why it requires an attached savings account. As the savings account grows, the policyholder gradually becomes more "self-insured" through the savings account built into the policy.

This analogy illustrates why term insurance is often called temporary coverage, and universal life and whole life permanent coverage. Although many people go through life just fine using term life insurance, others need permanent protection and may have reason to build up equity with life insurance.

Which Road to Take? Determining the Policy That's Right for You

Term life can be cost-effective for people with a need for pure life insurance for a specific period of time. Universal and whole life policies may be right for those who need to combine life insurance with a savings element or for those who have a lifetime need for insurance. Universal and whole life policies could be beneficial in providing estate liquidity, paying estate taxes, or paying the heirs of a key business partner in the event of the insured's death.

When deciding what's right for you, combine professional advice with your own research and, possibly, a second professional opinion. Then look at the options and make the decision that's best for you.

Read the following pages and weigh your options carefully to protect yourself from making a hasty decision that you may regret later. Ask informed questions and make your decision carefully: Most insurance companies offer a variety of contracts. Finally, it's important to purchase from a company with sterling ratings, which you can find out from any of the following ratings agencies:

▶ Standard & Poor's (http://www.standardpoors.com)
▶ Moody's Investor Service (http://www.moodys.com)
▶ Fitch IBCA (http://www.fitchibca.com)
▶ A.M. Best (http://www.ambest.com).

Remember, as with housing, cheapest isn't necessarily what you want or need in the long run. Meet with your financial advisor to analyze your needs and options. You're insuring the financial value of your life and protecting your spouse. When the resources are needed, they must be available. The following sections offer insight into how to choose the type of life insurance that may be best for your and your spouse's needs.

Route #1: Term Life Insurance

Term insurance offers the most coverage for the lowest premium and is the most economical if insurance is needed for a specific period of time, such as while you have a dependent spouse and children. Three popular types of term insurance are:

▶ Annual Renewable Term (ART)
▶ Level term
▶ Decreasing term or mortgage insurance

Each type serves different needs, so speak to your financial advisor or insurance broker about which type is right for your particular situation.

Advantages of term insurance. It's substantially less expensive than whole or universal life insurance and offers pure death protection. Some term policies can be renewed or converted, although usually at higher premiums.

Disadvantages of term insurance. There's no benefit if you outlive the specified period designated by the plan. And there's no savings element.

Route #2: Universal Life Insurance

Universal life insurance combines term life protection and a tax-deferred cash value fund that accumulates over time. This product and its cousin, variable universal life, are the insurance industry's answer to critics who suggest that consumers would be better off to buy term life insurance and invest the difference.

The life insurance company deducts certain expenses and the pure insurance protection cost from the premiums paid. The balance of the premium earns interest in a cash value fund, similar to a savings account.

Advantages of universal life insurance. These policies have a cash value that earns tax-deferred interest at competitive market rates. Moreover, premiums can be flexible, and you can skip payments as long as the accumulated cash value covers the cost of the pure insurance protection. Depending on the contract, you also may be able to increase or decrease the policy's survivor benefit according to your needs. Policy loans are also available at fairly competitive interest rates.

Disadvantages of universal life insurance. Interest rates paid by the insurance company may drop as low as the contract guaranteed rate, and you may have to pay additional premiums to keep the policy in force. Your contract also may not have the most competitive insurance interest rates or be the most effective savings vehicle.

Route #3: Variable Universal Life Insurance

Variable life insurance is like universal life in many ways, combining term life protection and a cash value fund. The big difference is that rather than earning a rate of interest, the cash portion can be invested in a variety of vehicles, such as equity and bond mutual funds, cash, and real estate securities. Unlike universal life, you choose the investments and assume the investment risk.

Advantages of variable universal life. You're guaranteed the minimum survivor benefit if the minimum required premium has been paid. You can change your investment allocation (the vehicles you have invested in), keep professional investment management, and enjoy tax-deferred earnings. There's also the potential that cash in the account will accumulate quickly due to equity growth.

Disadvantages of variable universal life insurance. Exposure to market risk may put your policy in jeopardy, forcing you to pay additional premiums to keep the contract in force. Also, your policy may not have the most competitive insurance rates and may not be the most cost-effective or flexible investment vehicle.

Route #4: Whole Life Insurance

Whole life insurance insures you for life. Some contracts are called "20-Pay Life" or "Life 65," which usually means the premiums are paid for 20 years or to age 65, respectively. The other types of whole life insurance are generally paid for your lifetime. The premium you pay the first month, quarter, or year remains the same for the entire term of the policy. Although premiums are initially higher than term or variable universal policies, whole life contracts come with many guarantees.

Advantages of whole life. Your premiums, interest, and survivor benefit are guaranteed and you have lifetime protection. The cash value of your policy includes the interest compounded over time, which can add substantially to your investment after about 10 years. You can get a policy loan at rates guaranteed in the contract. And you also derive forced, tax-deferred savings with the benefit of FIFO (first in, first out) withdrawals. Finally, if you need insurance protection for 10 or more years, this type of insurance may be cost-effective.

Disadvantages of whole life. Compared with term or universal plans, the premiums are higher and are not flexible. In addition, only guaranteed interest (not the current rate) is disclosed in the contract, and you should be prepared to pay the required premiums for at least 10 or more years.

Route #5: Partnership Life Insurance Plans

You might also consider insuring you and your spouse with a partnership plan. There are two types of plans: first-to-die and second-to-die. Both types insure two lives with one contract. They usually cost less than two individual policies and provide flexibility in the amount of premiums paid. The insurance carrier will blend dividend-paying whole life with term insurance. If you choose a blend that contains more whole life, the premiums will be higher versus a plan that has less whole life and more term insurance.

First-to-die plans work well for married couples or partners in personal or business relationships. The survivor benefit will be paid to the surviving partner upon the death of the first partner. If both partners die simultaneously, each partner's contingent beneficiary will be paid the full survivor benefit.

Second-to-die plans pay benefits after the death of the second or last surviving spouse and are often used to pay estate taxes. It's also a cost-effective way to fund and leverage a charitable gift. Premiums are based on the ages of both partners, and if one of you is in poor health or medically uninsurable, the good health of the other equalizes the underwriting risk.

Calculating the Toll: Cash Value Life Insurance vs. Other Investment Options

As mentioned above, the main difference between term and whole life is the savings element or cash value of the whole life policy. Because the cash value component is a long-term investment, it needs to be compared with other investment alternatives.

General Guidelines for Purchasing Life Insurance. When you're ready to buy, keep these general guidelines in mind:

▶ Buy insurance that covers the time frame corresponding with your exposure to risk. If you need death protection for a term of 30 years or less, term insurance may be your best option.

▶ Acquire the primary benefits of a whole life policy by buying term insurance and use the premium difference to pay off debt or invest in a Roth IRA.

▶ Consider using whole life insurance as a tax-sheltered investment vehicle if you have exhausted other tax-advantaged possibilities. These tax shelters include plans for retirement savings, such as a Roth IRA, traditional IRA, 401(k), and 403(b), which are discussed in detail in Chapter 4, and education savings plans, such as a 529 Plan or Education Savings Account, discussed in more detail in Chapter 6. You may also wish to compare whole life insurance with an annuity, another type of tax-sheltered investment vehicle, to determine which product—if either—is more appropriate for your circumstances.

▶ If you are unsure of your needs-based time frame, buy a convertible term policy that enables you to convert a traditional term policy to a whole life policy. Be aware, however, that a conversion option comes at a price.

▶ Purchase low-load or no-load insurance policies to minimize your insurance costs.

▶ Use the Internet to research options or work with an independent insurance consultant who represents a number of companies that provide high-quality, low-priced life insurance coverage. A quick check on competitive policies can be beneficial. Specific Web sites are listed in the Appendix.

When you have narrowed your search for the best policy to a few companies, you can use the "interest-adjusted net cost index" to help you make your final decision. This index, available for both term and cash value policies, factors in all the financial elements of an insurance policy, such as the company's dividend record, expenses, premium costs, and timing of payments. The result allows you to compare the prices of policies.

The index is expressed as a cost per $1,000 of insurance. For example, a policy with a $5 cost index costs $5 per $1,000 of coverage per year, or $500 for a $100,000 policy. These index costs range from a low of about $1 to as much as $10. Ask your insurance agent for the cost index of two or more comparable policies, even though the data may not be volunteered eagerly. The lower the cost index, the more insurance your money buys. Another objective source from which to obtain this data is *Consumer Reports*. Consult the most recent issue that examines life insurance.

From an investment perspective, life insurance is unique. The expected "return" on a life insurance policy is impossible to calculate. If you die prematurely, the return to your family is immeasurable. However, if you live a long and happy life, the numeric return may be minimal, but the peace of mind that comes from knowing your family will be able to live as you want them to is huge.

There are a few other life insurance facts you should be aware of: Life insurance is tax deferred during your lifetime; that is, you don't pay taxes on any earnings that accumulate and the face amount passes income tax free to your beneficiaries after your death. If you name a beneficiary other than your estate, the face amount of your life insurance policy passes directly to that beneficiary, which avoids the cost, delays, and potential publicity of the probate process.

No one enjoys talking about the possibility of unexpected death, but it does occur and should be planned for. You will be more comfortable after you go through the process and purchase the proper amount of coverage, knowing that your loved ones will be able to maintain their lifestyle if the unexpected happens.

▶ If Your Life's Journey Takes a Detour: Disability Insurance

Like life insurance, disability income insurance is designed to protect your income. If you have an accident or become ill and can't work, how much monthly disability income will you receive and for how long? Think of yourself as a money machine that provides the income that pays the bills. Insure yourself to the maximum allowed. The potential to earn income is your most significant asset. Although you might think it's highly unlikely that you will ever become disabled, either on the job or outside of work, you are mistaken. According to the Health Insurance Association of America, when you are age 40, for example, you have a 19 percent probability of suffering at least one disability lasting more than 90 days, but a disability can occur at any age.

If you work for a living and need your income to live on, you need disability insurance. Even if you and your spouse both work, the temporary loss of one of your incomes could be devastating financially, which would add to the physical and emotional problems you would probably experience because of the disability.

If you miss work for a short time, your employer will probably provide short-term sick leave. You might also collect benefits from workers' compensation if you are injured on the job. You may also be qualified to receive help from other government programs, such as veterans' benefits, civil service disability, black lung insurance for miners, and Medicaid for low-income people. If you are injured in a car accident, your auto insurance will pay you a certain amount of cash for a limited period of time. And if you are a union member, you might be eligible for group union disability coverage. You may also qualify for Social Security disability benefits if you become severely disabled. How much you receive depends on your salary and the number of years you have been covered by Social Security.

Even if you collect from several government programs, you and your spouse probably will not receive enough money to live comfortably. This is where individual long-term disability insurance becomes crucial. If you qualify, you can receive between 60 and 70 percent of your regular salary, depending on the policy, plus cost-of-living adjustments in some policies. The insurance companies do not pay 100 percent of your salary because they want you to have an incentive to go back to work.

What's the Toll? Financial Impact of Long-Term Disability

A disability can be more economically devastating than death. Not only does your income stop, but expenses usually increase. In addition, at almost any age, the chance of disability is far greater than the chance of death. If you are 35 to 65, the chances of a total disability of three months or more are 33 to 70 percent. Although the majority of disabilities are short in duration, nearly 30 percent of all cases are permanent. So ask yourself: What would happen financially to me and my family if I become disabled and can no longer work, for a few weeks or forever?

Even if your employer offers disability insurance, the coverage may not be enough to keep you and your spouse financially solvent. Self-employed people, of course, must obtain their own policies (more on that at the end of this section). And government programs provide few benefits. To receive Social Security, a worker must be totally and permanently disabled and be unable to work in any gainful activity anywhere in the country. These criteria make it notoriously difficult to collect benefits, and the amount collected is very low. Workers' compensation pays only for disabilities arising out of and in the course of employment.

So how much disability insurance do you need? Generally, as much as you can get, unless you have other sources of nonemployment income or investments to fall back on and you are willing to reduce your standard of living drastically. Insurers usually provide a maximum benefit of 60 to 70 percent of your income. If you pay for the policy, the benefits will be tax free; however, if your employer pays, your benefits are taxable. If your employer offers disability insurance and you are not automatically enrolled for it, sign up as soon as possible!

Coverage available under group disability plans is sometimes broader than that offered by individual policies, and the cost is usually a lot lower. Some group policies cannot be converted to individual policies. If you an-

Tollbooth 3.1

Example of Disability Insurance Costs

The cost of disability coverage, whether offered by a group or individual policy, depends on factors like occupation, age, sex, length of time for which benefits are payable, extent of coverage, size of benefits, and length of waiting period. If you're 30 to 40 years of age, the cost will probably be 2 to 3 percent of your gross annual income.

For example, if Bill, age 36, makes $50,000 a year, he will pay a $1,000 to $1,500 annual premium that will entitle him to a $30,000 to $32,500 annual benefit if he becomes disabled.

ticipate frequent job changes, worry about developing a condition that would make you ineligible for future coverage, or want to insure yourself more adequately, consider supplementing group coverage with an individual policy. Tollbooth 3.1 gives an example of the cost of disability insurance coverage.

Although paying disability premiums may seem expensive, especially because it's something you may never use, the peace of mind it brings can be well worth the cost of maintaining the policy. Although prices vary widely among disability policies, you can expect to pay about $1,000 a year for $12,000 worth of annual disability income coverage. Several types of insurance companies offer disability coverage; however, life insurers specialize in the product and will offer the best options at the lowest prices.

You probably will obtain a much better price and more generous benefits if you buy through a group plan. However, if you cannot purchase coverage through your employer, union, or trade association, it often makes sense to purchase an individual policy.

Finally, a specialized type of disability insurance is tied to your ability to repay loans. Banks, finance companies, car dealerships, and other lenders sell *credit disability insurance,* which covers your loan payments if you become disabled. Mortgage lenders push *mortgage disability insurance,* which makes your home payments if you have an accident or serious illness. In general, both credit and mortgage disability insurance policies are not good investments because they are overpriced. You will be better served by more comprehensive forms of disability coverage.

Get a Map: What to Look for When Buying a Disability Insurance Policy

Five features are critical in evaluating and selecting a disability income insurance policy. The following paragraphs describe each of them.

1. *Definitions of Disability.* Choose the most affordable policy that includes the broadest definition of what constitutes a disability. There are various ways to define disability, ranging from the inability to do any type of work to the difference in income between the work you were doing and what you are able to do after the disability. Check with your insurance agent to make certain you fully understand what is and is not a disability according to the terms of your policy.

2. *Elimination or Waiting Period.* The waiting period after the disability occurs and before benefits are paid is like a deductible, forcing the insured to bear part of the loss. Its purpose is to eliminate coverage for short-term, less serious disabilities. Frequently, elimination periods are 30, 60, 90, or 180 days. Therefore, you should choose a waiting period that is equal to the number of sick days you maintain at work, the length of any short-term disability coverage you may have, and the amount of your emergency savings.

3. *Monthly Benefit Payment.* Insurers typically limit coverage to 60 to 70 percent of monthly wages. Benefits of employer-paid policies are taxable.

4. *Maximum Benefit Period.* Benefits usually are payable until age 65 but can vary according to the cause of the disability.

5. *Renewal Provisions.* There are several renewal possibilities. Ranging from best to worst, they are

   - noncancelable
   - guaranteed renewable
   - conditionally renewable
   - renewable at a company's option
   - no renewal
   - cancelable

The following are a few other provisions and variables you should be aware of when shopping for disability insurance:

▶ *Guaranteed insurability.* This provision allows an individual whose income increases after the policy is purchased to increase the amount of coverage at specified dates after the inception of the policy, regardless of physical health.

▶ *Cost-of-living adjustment benefit.* This disability benefit increases annually, based on the Consumer Price Index or on a simple or compounded percentage specified in the policy. Policies using simple interest will cost less but may provide inadequate protection from inflation over longer periods, such as 20 years or more.

▶ *Additional insurance rider.* This feature is a variation on the cost-of-living rider and guaranteed insurability option that automatically increases policy benefits by 5 percent each year.

▶ *More choices.* Other options that can affect premiums and policy selection include a provision that allows you to obtain counseling or therapy; a presumptive disability clause, in which the loss of the use of two bodily members (both legs, for example), or the loss of sight is considered a total disability; residual and partial disability; rehabilitation provision; and exclusions.

▶ *Financial Strength of the Insurance Company.* Because a disability policy may pay benefits for 30 years or more, the financial strength of the company is an important factor in selecting a policy. A more expensive policy from a financially strong company may be a better deal than a cheaper one from a company that may not be around to pay the benefits.

▶ *Probation Period.* This is the period of time a policy must be in force before specified perils or illnesses are covered. This provision protects the insurance company from having to cover certain preexisting conditions and other adverse situations.

▶ *Disability Insurance for the Self-Employed.* If you're starting a business and are not already covered by an employer or individual policy, consider purchasing disability insurance while you're still employed. Once you are in business for yourself, you generally have to show a year's track record of income before you become eligible to purchase disability insurance. Even if you have disability coverage from an employer, consider a supplemental policy to help cover you after you leave the company.

Finally, before you buy disability insurance, make sure you understand all the provisions of your policy. The fine print may include clauses that make the policy a poor choice for you.

▶ Fit to Travel: Finding Affordable Health Insurance

Health insurance can't be taken for granted the way it used to be. More than 45 million Americans are not insured because they're not covered by their employers, they're unemployed, or they're self-employed, and they had deemed that the cost of health insurance premiums is prohibitively expensive for them. They're taking their chances that nothing catastrophic will happen to them. If you and your spouse are both lucky enough to have health insurance provided by your employers, then the only financial consideration is to determine which company's benefits are better for the money and then sign on with that one, an option you didn't have when you were single; you had to take whatever your company offered.

If, however, you are self-employed or need to secure your own policy for some other reason, compare your options carefully. You will most likely pay much more for health insurance when you become self-employed or retire than when you were employed, because most employers subsidize the cost of health insurance, paying 50 to 100 percent of the actual cost of their employees' insurance. Check out http://www.dol.gov/dol/topic/health-plans/index.htm. This interactive Web site is a resource to help employees and their families make informed decisions about their health benefits when facing life and work changes.

Consider membership in various associations, alumni or civic groups, churches, and professional or chamber of commerce organizations as a possible way to save money on health insurance. They may offer group policies, often at better rates than you can obtain on your own.

Fortunately, Congress passed a law called the Health Insurance Portability and Accountability Act of 1996 (also known as HIPAA or the Kennedy-Kasenbaum Bill), which allows people who have exhausted their COBRA benefits to obtain individual (nongroup) health insurance policies for themselves and their dependents without restrictions on preexisting conditions. Although Congress has guaranteed that you can get insurance, it has not mandated how much you pay for it.

The cost of health insurance depends on where you reside, your health history, and your age. Planning before you need insurance will allow you the most flexibility in determining the best options for health insurance coverage.

Therefore, you first need to decide your coverage needs, the monthly premium you can afford, the potential risk you will accept, and the health of your family. Then develop a checklist to compare different policies. On a blank sheet of paper, list the basic features, benefits, and costs down the left side of the page. At the top of the page, write the top three or four policies you're considering. Make a grid and check the appropriate box if a policy offers a particular feature and jot down the number or dollar figure as appropriate. Let's take a closer look at the various kinds of health insurance.

Another Fork in the Road: Fee-for-Service Plan, PPO, or HMO?

The individual health insurance market offers the same plans as the group market, including traditional fee-for-service arrangements, health maintenance organizations (HMOs), and preferred provider organizations (PPOs). Each plan has its own features.

Fee-For-Service Plans. Insurance companies pay fees to the insured for the services provided in these plans, which are also called indemnity plans. They offer the broadest choice of doctors and hospitals. Usually this type of insurance requires the insured to pay the provider up front for medical services, and then submit forms to the insurer to be reimbursed. You pay a monthly premium, an annual deductible (for each individual to be insured), and coinsurance after your deductible is met. (For example, your coinsurance may require you to pay 20 percent of the costs of medical treatment, and the insurer pays 80 percent). Most plans have caps, which limit the amount you will have to pay for medical bills in any one year, not including your premiums.

There are two types of coverage available in fee-for-service plans: (1) basic, which pays hospital room and care costs, surgery, and some doctor visits; and (2) major medical, which provides coverage for expensive treatments, subject to policy limits.

Health Maintenance Organizations (HMOs). These prepaid health plans are the least expensive and the least flexible. You pay a monthly premium, and the HMO provides comprehensive care for you and your family, including doctors' visits, hospital stays, emergency care, surgery, lab and X-rays, and preventive care. Usually your choice of doctors and hospitals is limited, and you may be assigned a doctor from those who have agreements with the HMO to provide care.

There may be a small co-payment ($10 or $20) for each doctor visit and a higher amount for emergency room treatment, but there are no claim forms to file. You may be assigned a physician or be allowed to choose one to serve as your primary care doctor. This doctor monitors your health and provides most of your health care, referring you to specialists only if needed.

Preferred Provider Organizations (PPOs). This plan combines the services of the other two plans. Like an HMO, a limited number of doctors and hospitals are available as preferred or in-network providers. You choose your own primary care doctor to monitor your health care and cover most preventive treatment. You can use doctors who are not part of the plan and still receive some coverage (referred to as out-of-network); however, you will pay a larger portion of the bill yourself. In addition, like a fee-for-service plan, a coinsurance percentage means that you will share the cost of your medical coverage.

Which Road to Take? Comparing Plans

If you are searching for a well-rounded plan, make sure that you are getting what you pay for. Read the fine print. Will your plan pay for X-rays? Will it cover your doctor's visit if you have the flu? Will it cover prescription drugs? Use a checklist of services to compare several policies. That checklist can include hospital care, doctor visits, and well-baby care, as well as the costs of premiums, deductibles, co-payments, maximum out-of-pocket expenses, and other options that are important to you.

Finding a cost-effective individual health policy can be tricky. Talk to other people in the same circumstances as you. You can contact a licensed independent insurance agent or broker in your area who specializes in individual health policies, or you can begin your research online. Internet sources include the following:

- ► http://www.nase.org
- ► http://www.healthinsurance.org
- ► http://www.ehealthinsurance.com
- ► http://www.insure.com

▶ The Journey Home: Protecting One of Your Biggest Assets

If you own a home, it's probably your largest single asset, but it's also a potential source of a liability claim against you. Therefore, it's important to have adequate homeowners insurance coverage for damage and liability claims. You should work with a trusted insurance professional and have a basic understanding of homeowners coverage.

Big Bumps in the Road: Home Insurance Covers Certain Perils

Most homeowners policies cover 12 basic "named perils:" fire, lightning, windstorm, hail, theft, aircraft, vehicles, vandalism and malicious mischief, explosions, volcanic eruption, riot or civil commotion, and smoke. "Broad named perils" include the following:

- ▶ falling objects
- ▶ weight of ice, snow, and sleet
- ▶ accidental discharge or overflow of water or stream
- ▶ sudden and accidental tearing apart, cracking, burning, or bulging of steam from plumbing, heating, or air conditioning system
- ▶ damage from a hot water, air-conditioning, or automatic fire protective sprinkler system, or from within a household appliance
- ▶ freezing of a plumbing, heating, air conditioning, or automatic fire sprinkler system or of a household appliance
- ▶ sudden and accidental damage from an artificially generated electrical current

General Exclusions. Although all of the above are generally covered, homeowners policies also have eight general exclusions that prohibit coverage for a loss. (It's possible to buy riders to cover some of these exclusions). These exclusions include the following:

1. ordinance or law (condemnation)
2. earth movement (earthquake)
3. water damage (flood)
4. neglect (abandonment)
5. intentional loss (any intentional damage)

6. nuclear hazard
7. power failure (interruption of power)
8. war

Get Out of the Ditch and Back on the Road: Know What Your Insurance Covers

Each homeowners insurance policy has a property and a liability section. Let's look at what is covered within each section.

Dwelling and Other Structures. Base your coverage amount on the replacement cost of your home, excluding the value of the land. "Other structures coverage" is generally a set percentage of the cost of the coverage for the home itself. At a minimum, your mortgage company will require the coverage amount to match or exceed your mortgage loan balance.

Personal Property. Coverage is generally a set percentage of the cost of the building, with limited coverage for jewelry, firearms, silver, computers, artwork, and other extras. You can get additional coverage with a rider/endorsement (addition) to your policy or a separate personal property floater policy.

Loss of Use. This provision covers the increase in your housing costs if your property is temporarily uninhabitable.

Personal Liability. This feature protects you and your family from the cost of legal actions or claims for injuries or property damage by people other than those who reside in the home. You should have at least $100,000 in coverage, and $300,000 is commonly recommended. Depending on your other assets, even more may be advisable. More can be purchased through a separate umbrella liability policy.

Medical Payments. This pays the cost of minor accidental injuries occurring on your property and minor injuries caused by you, your family, or pets without determining fault. Coverage from $1,000 to $5,000 is provided by most policies.

How Claims Are Settled. The standard claims settlement method is the actual cash value method (current replacement value less depreciation), but consider getting replacement cost coverage. This option allows you to have a loss replaced at the current market value. Maintain your building coverage at 100 percent of the replacement cost, and keep in mind periodic increases in coverage to compensate for the rising costs of material and labor as well as rising property values.

Keep Good Records. In your safe deposit box, keep a detailed home inventory supported by pictures or a video as adequate evidence to support your claim in case of loss.

▶ Don't Leave Home Without an Umbrella! Additional Insurance Options

Personal umbrella insurance is additional liability coverage to protect you from catastrophic financial losses that could wipe out assets. It fits over your auto and homeowners insurance policies like an umbrella (hence the name) to provide additional coverage payable after your primary insurance coverage is exhausted.

Suppose you're having a dinner party in your home, and a guest falls and has a major injury. Your homeowners insurance will pay the liability on the claim up to its $100,000 limit. But suppose your guest sues you for $1 million. How do you pay the other $900,000? The answer is with an umbrella insurance policy, which typically comes in increments of $1 million to $5 million, and is reasonably priced, perhaps $200 to $300 a year for $1 million in liability coverage. An umbrella policy may cover your home, auto, boat, aircraft, and other nonbusiness assets, and it protects you from the need to pay damages to other people, including bodily injury, mental anguish, shock, sickness, disease, disability, false arrest, false imprisonment, wrongful eviction, detention, libel, defamation of character, and invasion of privacy.

Umbrella insurance does not, however, cover your obligation for workers' compensation and disability benefits, your property damages, or product failure.

How to Buy It. Umbrella insurance usually is available through your current insurance provider or another company. If you opt for a stand-alone policy, you should not need to move your homeowners or auto insurance. To alleviate any gaps in liability coverage, make sure your auto and homeowners insurance policies have coverage up to the deductible on the umbrella policy.

Your insurance professional or financial planner can help you determine the right amount of coverage. A general guideline: Round up your net worth to the next million.When you realize that you can be sued for everything you have, it pays to insure your entire net worth, especially when the premiums are generally so affordable.

If You're an "Armchair Traveler": Insurance for Home-Based Businesses

If you or your spouse runs a home-based business, you probably need extra insurance protection for all your equipment. Most homeowner's policies provide only a few thousand dollars in coverage for property used for business purposes. Therefore, acquire an endorsement, or an additional clause that specifies particular items, to cover your computers, fax machines, office furniture, copiers, file cabinets, and other equipment.

Many insurance companies offer policies at special rates that are tailored to cover small businesses. Usually homeowner's policies do not cover liabilities arising from business activities. For example, you would not be covered if a delivery person who falls on your property while delivering a package for your business files a suit against you. However, a *small business specialty policy* insures against such an event. You might also investigate *business interruption insurance,* which pays for your temporary relocation to other quarters while your office is being repaired due to a fire or another disaster.

Detour: Renters and Condo Owners also Need Insurance

Although your landlord's insurance covers the building you live in, you should buy a separate policy to cover your possessions if you rent. The provisions of a renter's policy are nearly identical to those of homeowner's coverage. You are protected against loss or damage from the most common perils, such as fire, explosion, water damage, and vandalism or theft. If you own valuables, such as jewelry or computers, you probably need a rider to provide coverage beyond the typical limits. Most renter's policies impose a $1,000 limit on jewelry, $3,000 to $10,000 on computers, and $2,500 to $10,000 on silverware. As with homeowners insurance, it is best to buy replacement cost coverage rather than a policy based on cash value.

In addition to property coverage, most renter's policies provide liability insurance if someone claims injury due to your negligence. For example, bodily injury liability pays medical costs, as well as your legal defense fees if you injure or kill someone accidentally.

Insurance for condominium owners is similar to coverage available for renters. The condominium association buys insurance that protects the buildings, grounds, and common areas, and each owner must obtain special condominium coverage for the contents of their apartments, walls that are not shared with other apartments, and other things that are not commonly owned, as well as liability claims.

▶ Estimate Your Tolls: Take Inventory of the Assets in Your Home

Keeping all of the preceding guidelines in mind, determine how much home-owners insurance you need. First, take a household inventory to see what actually needs to be insured. Walk around your home; list each item you own on an inventory sheet, record the amount you paid for it, and how much it would cost to replace it. Make sure that you also note model and serial numbers. If you have no idea what things cost today, you might consider bringing in an appraiser to help you. Roadmap 3.1, divided into sections according to the rooms in your house, will help you inventory the contents of your home. Couples who are just getting married will find this process easier, because many of your household possessions may be brand new, so it will be easier to record the purchase and replacement prices.

In addition to listing your household possessions, photograph or video-tape the contents of each room. If you videotape, talk about the objects you are taping and estimate how much they cost. Keep the pictures or tape some-where other than at your home (at work or a friend's home or safe deposit box) so that you will have access to it if your house is destroyed or damaged. These physical records can be invaluable if you ever file a claim and have to convince an insurance adjuster that you owned a particular item. The records will also help you declare the value of your property.

Reducing Your Toll: Minimizing Your Premium

The best way to qualify for the lowest insurance rates is to guard against ac-cidents, thefts, and losses. Taking some of the more obvious precautions can often qualify you for direct discounts. These actions include the following:

▶ Install deadbolt locks on doors and key locks on windows. If your home or apartment is at street level, add grates or grilles to protect windows.

Roadmap 3.1

Household Inventory Worksheet

Article and Description	Purchase Price	Replacement Cost	Total Purchase Cost	Total Replacement Cost
Bathrooms				
Carpets/Rugs	$_____	$_____		
Clothes Hampers	_____	_____		
Curtains	_____	_____		
Dressing Tables	_____	_____		
Electrical Appliances	_____	_____		
Lighting Fixtures	_____	_____		
Linens	_____	_____		
Scales	_____	_____		
Shower Curtains	_____	_____		
Other	_____	_____		
Total for Bathrooms			$_____	$_____
Bedrooms				
Beds/Mattresses	$_____	$_____		
Books/Bookcases	_____	_____		
Carpets/Rugs	_____	_____		
Chairs	_____	_____		
Clocks	_____	_____		
Clothing	_____	_____		
Curtains/Drapes	_____	_____		
Desks/Dressers	_____	_____		
Jewelry	_____	_____		
Lamps	_____	_____		
Mirrors	_____	_____		
Plants	_____	_____		
Records/Tapes/CDs	_____	_____		
Stereos/Radios	_____	_____		
Tables	_____	_____		
TV/Computers	_____	_____		
Wall Hangings/Pictures	_____	_____		
Wall Units	_____	_____		
Other	_____	_____		
Total for Bedrooms			$_____	$_____
Dining Room				
Buffets	$_____	$_____		
Carpets/Rugs	_____	_____		
Chairs	_____	_____		

Article and Description	Purchase Price	Replacement Cost	Total Purchase Cost	Total Replacement Cost
Dining Room (cont'd)				
China	_____	_____		
Clocks	_____	_____		
Curtains/Drapes	_____	_____		
Glassware	_____	_____		
Lamps/Fixtures	_____	_____		
Silverware	_____	_____		
Tables	_____	_____		
Wall Hangings/Pictures	_____	_____		
Other	_____	_____		
Total for Dining Room			$_____	$_____
Garage/Basement/Attic				
Furniture	$_____	$_____		
Ladders	_____	_____		
Lawn Mowers	_____	_____		
Luggage	_____	_____		
Shovels	_____	_____		
Snowblowers	_____	_____		
Sports Equipment	_____	_____		
Sprinklers/Hoses	_____	_____		
Tools/Supplies	_____	_____		
Toys	_____	_____		
Washer/Dryer	_____	_____		
Wheelbarrows	_____	_____		
Work Benches	_____	_____		
Other	_____	_____		
Total for Garage/ Basement/Attic			$_____	$_____
Kitchen				
Buffets	$_____	$_____		
Cabinets	_____	_____		
Chairs	_____	_____		
Clocks	_____	_____		
Curtains	_____	_____		
Dishes	_____	_____		
Dishwasher	_____	_____		
Disposal/Trash Compactor	_____	_____		
Food/Supplies	_____	_____		
Freezer	_____	_____		
Glassware	_____	_____		
Lighting Fixtures	_____	_____		
Refrigerator	_____			

Article and Description	Purchase Price	Replacement Cost	Total Purchase Cost	Total Replacement Cost
Kitchen (cont'd)				
Pots/Pans	_____	_____		
Radio/Television	_____	_____		
Small Appliances	_____	_____		
Stove	_____	_____		
Tables	_____	_____		
Washer/Dryer	_____	_____		
Other	_____	_____		
Total for Kitchen			$ _____	$ _____
Living Room				
Books/Bookcases	$ _____	$ _____		
Carpets/Rugs	_____	_____		
Chairs	_____	_____		
Clocks	_____	_____		
Curtains/Drapes	_____	_____		
Desks	_____	_____		
Lamps	_____	_____		
Mirrors	_____	_____		
Musical Instruments	_____	_____		
Plants	_____	_____		
Records/Tapes/CDs	_____	_____		
Sofas	_____	_____		
Stereo/Radio	_____	_____		
Tables	_____	_____		
Television	_____	_____		
Wall Hangings/Pictures	_____	_____		
Wall Units	_____	_____		
Other	_____	_____		
Total for Living Room			$ _____	$ _____
Porch/Patio				
Carpets/Rugs	$ _____	$ _____		
Chairs	_____	_____		
Lamps	_____	_____		
Outdoor Cooking Equipment	_____	_____		
Outdoor Furniture	_____	_____		
Plants/Planters	_____	_____		
Tables	_____	_____		
Other	_____	_____		
Total for Porch/Patio			$ _____	$ _____
TOTAL HOUSEHOLD			$ _____	$ _____

▶ Install a burglar alarm system that attaches to doors and windows, and rings loudly if activated. Make sure that it automatically notifies the local police department or alarm company if there is an intruder.

▶ Keep wiring in top condition.

▶ Maintain stairs, railings, carpets, and flooring to minimize the possibility of falls.

▶ Keep fresh batteries in smoke detectors and install a sprinkler system and fire alarm that automatically alerts the fire department when the detector senses smoke.

▶ Install exterior lights to make it difficult for a burglar to work in secrecy.

In addition, most companies shave your premiums if you are a longtime customer who has never filed a claim, and if you have policies for auto or life insurance with the same company.

Rates on homeowners policies are also based on the neighborhood in which your home is located. Obviously, owners of homes in crime-infested areas will pay higher premiums than those whose neighborhoods boast tight security and few crimes. Also, the closer your home is to fire and police protection, the lower your premiums will be. In general, newer homes qualify for lower rates than older homes because older buildings deteriorate over time and are more likely to have problems with their wiring, plumbing, and heating systems.

Another way to cut your premiums is to accept higher deductibles. Even when you agree to a substantial deductible, however, you gain protection against the enormous losses that homeowners insurance is designed to cover.

▶ "Baby on Board": How Insurance Changes When You Have Kids

When you have a child, you may need to increase your life insurance, disability insurance, and health insurance coverage. Selecting the right policy and amount of insurance can buy you the comfort of knowing that your family will be financially stable when you die. As discussed in the life insurance section earlier in this chapter, you have several options as to the type of life insurance you purchase: term life, whole life, variable life, universal life, and so on. A term life policy is typically the best for most young, middle-income families with children, because it has affordable premiums at a set rate and can be purchased to cover a specific period of time.

It's also time to review your disability coverage. During your prime earning years, ages 35 to 65, you are more likely to become unable to work because of illness or injury than you are to die. Disability insurance guarantees you a portion of your salary (usually 60 to 70 percent) if you cannot work.

Many health care plans have agreements with doctors, hospitals, and other facilities that offer favorable terms if you use their preferred providers. Become familiar with your health insurance coverage before you have your baby (if you are planning a family), so that you get the most out of your prenatal, maternity, and postnatal care. Knowing how to properly use your health care benefits can save you hundreds of dollars in medical costs. Fortunately, many health insurance plans have special coverage for babies, which includes well-baby care. Read and understand your insurance documents so you know the procedure on when and how to add your baby to your policy.

► The End of the Journey: Merging Insurance with Your Estate Plans

Purchasing a life insurance policy is a very safe way to build an asset over time to provide for a beneficiary or to make sure your executor will have the money necessary to help pay your estate's probate costs, debts, and taxes. The proceeds from your life insurance policy may also be exempt from your state's inheritance tax (if your state has inheritance tax and only if it's either a tiny policy or if paid to a spouse only).

As long as the beneficiary of your life insurance policy is not your estate, the policy proceeds will not go through probate when you die. Therefore, they will be available immediately after your death. However, if your estate is the policy beneficiary, the insurance proceeds will be probated.

Another potential drawback of making your estate the beneficiary of a life insurance policy is that the proceeds will be subject to the claims of creditors to whom you may owe money at the time of your death. However, in most states, the proceeds will be protected from these claims if you make the policy payable to your spouse, a dependent, or a trust established for the benefit of someone else. Your estate attorney can tell you how your state treats life insurance proceeds.

The main disadvantage of using an insurance policy as an estate planning tool is its lack of flexibility. For example, as the policyholder, you cannot specify when the beneficiary of your policy should receive the policy proceeds or how the proceeds will be paid, whether in a lump sum, a series of payments, or in some other way.

Another way to provide financially for your children in the event of your death is to make them the beneficiary of your insurance policy, employee benefits plan, or IRAs. After your death, the proceeds from these assets, the survivor benefits, will automatically pass directly to your children, avoiding probate and the claims of creditors.

If your minor children are the beneficiaries of your life insurance policy or annuity, the survivor benefits they are entitled to won't be released until a *property guardian* (the adult you appoint to manage the benefits) or another adult with legal authority has been chosen to manage these funds on your children's behalf. If the benefits are placed in a trust, the adult will be a trustee. If the benefits are deposited in a custodial account under the Uniform Gifts to Minors Act or the Uniform Transfers to Minors Act, the adult in charge of those assets will be an *account custodian*. (See Chapter 5 for more information about this issue and estate planning in general.).

▶ On the Road the Second Time Around: Protecting Children from a Prior Marriage

Most married people leave all of their estate to the surviving spouse. However, if you do this and if either of you has children from a previous marriage, you have no guarantee that your spouse will plan an estate that will leave at least some of those assets to your children, especially if your spouse also has children from a former marriage. And if your spouse and children do not get along, you may have real cause for concern.

There are several ways to deal with this potential problem.

1. You and your spouse can coordinate the provisions of your wills to provide for one another and for any children that each of you has from a previous marriage. Because each of you can change or revoke your wills at any time, however, you run the risk that your spouse's will could be changed, leaving nothing to your children.

2. You can purchase a life insurance policy, name your children as policy beneficiaries, and set up an irrevocable life insurance trust. To make this option work, your beneficiaries, not you, must own the policy. In other words, the policy must be in their names, not yours. Because they are children, you will have to give them enough money each year to pay the insurance premiums.

3. You can establish a trust. Your attorney can help you set up a trust that will provide for your spouse until his or her death followed by the transfer of trust assets to your children.

4. You can negotiate a legally binding prenuptial agreement before you get married or a postnuptial agreement after you are married. The agreement can spell out exactly how each of you will divide up your estates after your deaths, including what you will leave to your children.

All of these options should be discussed frankly and openly at the outset to avoid potential problems later on your journey together.

Seeing the World in an RV

Retirement Planning

Achieving financial security in your retirement years has never been more important—even if you're still in your twenties and retirement is decades away. More people than ever before are living into their eighties, nineties, and beyond. At the same time, many budget-cutting corporations are nudging (and, in some cases, pushing) their employees to accept early retirement packages.

The only solution to the coming retirement crunch is to understand your options, plan carefully to meet your goals, and follow through on your plan. The key to achieving a financially secure retirement is to start early. The younger you begin, the more you capitalize on your biggest ally, time. If you make the magic of compounding interest work for you while you are in your twenties or thirties rather than in your forties or fifties, you will have a much better chance of amassing the capital you need to live on in retirement.

To give you a dramatic example, let's say that starting at age 30, you earn $30,000 a year and save only 6 percent of your salary each month, or $150. If you earn a 10 percent average annual return, you will end up with $574,242 by the time you reach age 65! In contrast, if you start saving at age 55, assuming all other variables remain constant, you will reap only $30,983 over the next 10 years. Although retirement is probably the furthest thought from most people's minds when they are young, you can see that investing a small amount of money wisely can yield an enormous payoff.

Employers and the government are both increasingly trying to reduce their obligation to support you in retirement. Companies have become stingier about offering the traditionally defined benefit pension plan, which employees do not contribute to.

Today employers often replace the pension plan with a defined contribution profit-sharing plan, which may or may not include a 401(k) salary reduction plan. 401(k) plans only benefit employees who contribute some of their salary. The federal government, weighed down by trillions of dollars of debt, is in no position to support sizable increases in Social Security benefits and probably will reduce them as more baby boomers enter retirement. Therefore, given that cutbacks in retirement income are likely to continue in the future, your actions to build your savings and investments will be largely responsible for the quality of your retirement.

So even though you're just getting married and starting out on your new life together, and you have many other financial issues to consider and decisions to make, it's also important at this time to discuss with your spouse when you both want to retire, how you want to spend your retirement, and what that lifestyle might cost. Because this book focuses on finance, this chapter won't get into lifestyle decisions, such as whether you should move to Florida, Arizona, or a retirement community. Instead, we'll focus on how to figure out the amount of money you'll need when you retire, and how you can start saving and investing now to meet these goals. Let's hit the road!

▶ Stay on Course: What to Expect from Your Company-Sponsored Retirement Plans

No matter how much Social Security you may qualify for, it will clearly not be enough to maintain a comfortable standard of living as your sole source of income. You will need other resources to enhance your retirement lifestyle. Much of this information may already be familiar to you, but it seems appropriate to provide a refresher course at this stage of your life, when you're merging your finances and making new financial plans.

Two forms of company-sponsored retirement plans exist: one that your employer provides without any contribution from you, and one to which you contribute part of your earnings during your working years. If your employer does not fund a retirement plan for you, you should build your own retirement fund through a consistent savings strategy.

Defined Benefit Plans

If you or your spouse work for a company, government agency, or nonprofit organization that provides a traditional defined benefit pension plan, consider yourself lucky—presuming you plan to stay there until retirement or at least for many years. Many companies are cutting back or eliminating these plans because they are expensive to fund and administer. For this reason and because you may change jobs many times between now and retirement, you and/or your spouse should not assume that you will receive a defined benefit pension upon retirement.

However, for employees who qualify, defined benefit plans can provide a substantial portion (from 10 to 40 percent) of your total retirement income. The amount you receive often depends on the number of years you worked for your employer and the amount of your salary in your last few years at the company. The longer you worked for the employer and the higher your salary, the fatter your monthly pension check.

The size of your pension benefit should be a factor in your decision to leave one employer for another. Every time you hook up with a new company, you start at square one in accumulating pension credits. The pension benefit you receive from your former employer is locked at the level earned when you left the company. If you leave your present company for another, you may be offered the option to receive your pension benefit in a *lump sum,* which can be rolled over into the new firm's plan or an IRA. When you accept a lump sum, you receive an amount that is discounted into today's dollars based on an assumed rate of return. Ask your employer what this rate of return is. If you think you can beat the return by investing on your own, consider taking the lump sum. You must be extremely careful to make sure that any lump sum is deposited directly into an IRA through a *trustee-to-trustee transfer,* or the IRS will withhold 20 percent of the cash. However, if you fear that you won't do as well, or if you like the security of knowing that you will have a portion of your retirement income that you can never outlive, you might leave the money with your employer's plan.

The decision to take all of your pension money at once is extremely complicated, so consult a qualified financial planner before you grab what may look like a huge chunk of cash. In many cases, you have no option in taking a lump sum. You must wait until retirement age to begin drawing payments from the plan. If, by chance, you return to a former employer, you will again earn pension credits. Depending on how long you were away, you may not be penalized much for your absence. In any case, for most people who will depend on that monthly pension check, it is far safer to opt for an annuity than to take on the responsibility of investing the lump sum.

Defined Contribution Plans

If your employer does not offer a traditional defined benefit pension plan, it probably offers a defined contribution plan, which gives you the opportunity to put aside money from your salary on a tax-deferred basis until you retire. Unlike a benefit plan, a contribution plan does not obligate your company to pay a certain pension benefit. Instead, you may set aside a certain contribution, which your employer may or may not match. Either way, however, you must choose among various investment options. This decision makes you responsible for the ultimate size of your retirement benefit. Like income from all other retirement plans, investment earnings from defined contribution plans grow tax deferred.

Your company may make its contributions to your plan in cash, which you can allocate among various investment options. Or it may give you company stock, which you can hold onto or possibly sell. Some companies offer a combination of cash and stock. The amount of your company's contribution is determined either by a percentage of its profits, in which case it is called a *profit-sharing plan,* or by a percentage of your salary, in which case it is called a *money purchase plan.* In a profit-sharing plan, when the firm has a profitable year, you might receive as much as an additional 10 to 15 percent of your salary in your defined contribution account. But when profits fall or the company suffers a loss, you may get 5 percent or less, or possibly no contribution at all.

To qualify for participation in a company's plan, you usually must work there at least one year. Once you start contributing to the plan, many companies give you a matching contribution. Some companies will contribute only if you participate in this option. Their match may be as generous as 100 percent or as little as 10 percent. A more typical match is 25 to 50 percent. For example, if you set aside 6 percent of your salary in such a plan, the company would kick in another 3 percent every year. Few investments offer this type of an instant 50 percent return, so take advantage of this option, to the maximum amount!

Any money that you contribute to a defined contribution plan is always vested, meaning that you can take it with you or roll it over into another firm's plan or an IRA if you change employers. However, to provide you with an incentive to stay, most firms make you wait three to five years before their contributions are fully vested.

Salary Reduction Plans: 401(k)s and Their Kin

The most common type of defined contribution plan is a *salary reduction plan*. If you work for a private company, it's called a 401(k) plan, named for the obscure section of the IRS code that permits it. On the other hand, if you work for a tax-exempt organization, such as a religious, educational, or charitable group, it's called a *403(b) plan*. State and local government workers are offered *457 plans*, and federal employees can sign up for the *federal thrift savings fund*. Although these plans are all different, they work basically the same way.

In each of the plans mentioned, your employer deducts a percentage of your salary (usually between 2 and 25 percent, according to your wishes) and deposits the funds in your plan account. The money is deducted from your salary before being taxed at the federal, state, or local level, but after Social Security taxes are deducted. As a result, the earnings you report to the IRS are lessened by the amount of your annual contribution. The money you set aside, whether or not it is matched by your employer, is invested in a range of stock, bond, and money market options, and all investment earnings accumulate tax deferred. You pay taxes only when you withdraw the money at retirement.

If you don't understand these options or don't take advantage of a 401(k) plan through your employer, you're not alone. More than 70 percent of Americans with the option to open a 401(k) account at work do not understand or fully utilize this fantastic wealth-building program.

For most people, a 401(k) is the main retirement option. Your money grows on a tax-deferred basis until you retire, and then you pay taxes on withdrawals at your post-retirement income tax rate. The benefits of a 401(k) as a savings vehicle include immediate tax savings on contributions, tax-deferred growth of investment earnings, and the possibility of free money in the form of matching contributions from your employer. Let's take a closer look at the benefits of these plans.

▶ *Benefit 1: Immediate Tax Savings.* Keeping the 401(k)'s tax-deferred earnings in mind, let's say you invest $100 per month annually in your company's plan. Assuming you're in the 28 percent tax bracket, that's a little more than $320 in annual taxes owed on the money if it's not contributed to the plan. In other words, your $1,200 annual investment in the 401(k) really costs you only about $880 when you account for the tax savings! (See Roadmap 4.1.) Or, let's look at it another way. To net $1,200 after taxes to invest outside the 401(k), you must earn $1,524, assuming a 28 percent tax bracket. In other words, you need $324 more to achieve the same result! To learn more about how pretax contributions can affect your take-home pay, visit http://www.401k.com/401k/tools/takehomepay/ takehomepay.htm.

▶ *Benefit 2: Tax-Deferred Growth.* Because interest and dividends in a 401(k) are tax-deferred, they compound tax free until the investment is withdrawn. Over time, the gap between the value of a taxable and a tax-deferred account earning the same rate of return increases sharply.

▶ *Benefit 3: The Employer's Match.* One of the greatest advantages of a 401(k) is that many employers contribute to their employees' 401(k)s by matching a portion of the money contributed by the employee. For example, for each $100 you contribute to the plan, your employer may add $50 to your account, giving you a total of $150. That's an immediate 50 percent return on your out-of-pocket $100 investment! No tax advantage gives you a better deal.

A tip for those who currently earn more than $95,000 a year: Be aware of your contribution percentage. If it's too high and you contribute the maximum amount before year's end, you could miss out on a portion of your employer's match, so talk to your employee benefits office. The law allows a maximum annual contribution of $15,000 for 2006 ($20,000 if you're age 50 or over).

If a 401(k) plan is available, do whatever you can to invest in it, even if it's only a nominal amount from each paycheck. Tollbooth 4.1 shows how you can calculate the percentage of your income that you should contribute to your 401(k) in order to meet your financial goals.

Roadmap 4.1

Saving in a Tax-Deferred Retirement Account vs. a Taxable Account

This chart shows the results* if you invested $100 a month in a tax-deferred retirement plan versus a taxable investment, subject to a 28 percent federal income tax rate.

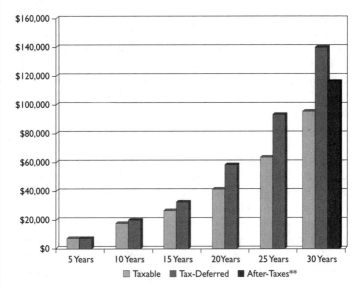

*Investment assumes the following: an annual effective 8 percent return, no changes to principal, and no change to the income tax rate.

**Tax-deferred investment after taxes. Although accumulations in a tax-deferred retirement plan are for retirement, we have illustrated the taxes you would pay on a lump-sum withdrawal after 30 years, given the assumptions. Payout options over time can spread out tax liability.

Tollbooth 4.1

Maximizing Your Employer's 401(k) Match

This worksheet can help you determine how much of your salary to contribute to your 401(k) plan to maximize your employer's match.

A. Enter your annual salary. $_____

B. Enter the number of pay periods.   _____

C. Calculate your pay per period:
   Divide A by B.   A ÷ B = $_____

D. Enter your desired annual contribution. $_____

E. Calculate your contribution per pay period:
   Divide D by B.   D ÷ B = $_____

F. Calculate the contribution's percentage of pay:
   Divide E by C.   E ÷ C =   0._____

G. Multiply F by 100 to determine
   percentage of pay.   F × 100 = _____%

The IRS limits the amount that you can contribute annually to your salary reduction plan, though it increases slightly each year because of inflation. Although you should always try to contribute the maximum that your employer matches, you can add extra cash to boost you to the maximum if you can afford it. However, the IRS mandates that you cannot invest more than the lesser of 25 percent of your salary or $42,000 (as of 2005) into all company savings plans combined. The maximum contribution to all defined benefit pensions is based on income up to $210,000 (as of 2005), which may limit how much you can contribute to various retirement plans.

Once you see the money accumulate steadily in your account, you must allocate it among the various investment options presented. Some plans allow you to switch from one option to another every day if you wish, while others limit you to quarterly or annual shifts. You usually receive quarterly written reports describing your funds' progress, and you can call the plan's representatives to learn the status of your account.

Usually you will choose among various stock funds, bond funds, or funds that combine stocks and bonds. Each category may offer many options. For example, among stock funds, you may be able to select aggressive, international, equity income, or index funds (funds based on common stock indexes, such as the Dow Jones or Standard & Poor's). Among bond funds, you may be offered government, corporate, international, or junk bond funds (funds invested in bonds considered risky). Some combined stock and bond options might include balanced funds and asset allocation funds. In addition, most salary reduction plans offer money market funds, company stock, and *guaranteed investment contracts* (GICs), which are similar to certificates of deposit (CDs). GICs pay a fixed rate for a set time, usually one to five years, and they are backed by the insurance company or bank that issued them.

When deciding how to spread your money among investment options, assess your tolerance for risk (discussed in more detail in the next section), and balance that factor with the length of time until you and your spouse will need the money. Then look at how you have allocated your money outside of your salary reduction plan. If you hold mostly conservative bonds and CDs, you may want to invest more retirement plan money in aggressive options. On the other hand, if you possess a large portfolio of aggressive stocks and mutual funds outside of your salary reduction plan, you might want to put more of your pension money in conservative assets. In general, the younger you are, the more money you should invest in growth-oriented options. In the long run, growth-oriented vehicles like aggressive stock funds will outperform stodgy fixed income bonds and GICs. The biggest mistake that many people make is to sink most or all of their retirement plan money in money market accounts, GICs, or bonds, thus depriving themselves of the opportunity for significant long-term gains from stocks.

As a rule of thumb, invest 60 to 80 percent or more of your defined contribution money in stock funds while you are in your twenties, thirties, and forties. As you enter your late forties and early fifties and into the early years of retirement, cut that percentage to between 50 and 60 percent.

Withdrawing cash from a salary reduction plan before retirement. Don't withdraw money from your salary reduction plan unless you desperately need it and have no other sources of funds. If you find you must obtain these assets, you have two ways of tapping your account. The better way is to borrow against your accumulated assets. Most plans allow you to borrow for whatever purpose you like; and others let you borrow only for a major expense, such as the down payment on a home or your children's tuition bills. Usually you can borrow up to half the value of your account balance or $50,000, whichever is less, though some companies impose lower maximums. You normally have up to five years to repay the loan through payroll deduction.

Hazard!

Don't Invest Too Much in Your Own Company

If you invest your retirement savings in stocks, don't sink too much money into the stock of the company you work for. If your company matches your contributions to your company pension plan in company stock, you will surely benefit if the firm does well. But as wonderful as your company's prospects may be, you do not want to have too high a concentration of your plan's assets in your own company in case it runs into trouble.

Most companies charge an interest rate either equal to or slightly above the prime lending rate. Because this loan is considered consumer interest, it is usually not tax deductible. If you leave your company while the loan remains outstanding, you must repay it, or the money due will be deducted from your account balance and taxes and penalties will be due.

The other, less advantageous way to tap your salary reduction plan is to withdraw funds. To receive the money at all, however, you must prove that you suffer from a financial hardship. This means that you have no other way of raising the money to pay expenses such as huge medical bills for which you cannot be reimbursed, post-secondary school tuition payments, a home, or funds to prevent foreclosure or eviction. If you qualify for one of these hardships, you still must pay a 10 percent penalty on all withdrawals if you are younger than age 59½, as well as income taxes in the year you receive the funds. In addition, you forfeit all the tax-deferred compounding of investment interest and capital gains you would have earned if you had left the money in the account. Unless you find yourself in an extreme situation, it is therefore far better to borrow against your account balance than to withdraw from it.

If You're Driving the Bus: Pension Plans for the Self-Employed

When you are self-employed, no one looks out for your interests except you. Because you do not have the luxury of working for a company that offers a defined benefit or defined contribution plan, you must take a more active role in funding your retirement. If you never set up one of the pension plans that the IRS code allows, you and your spouse will have to survive on only your personal investments and Social Security, if it's available, when you retire (and your spouse's pension, if there is one).

If you or your spouse are self-employed, either full-time or part-time, you can contribute to either a Keogh plan, a *simplified employee pension plan* (SEP), a SIMPLE IRA, or a one-person 401(k) plan. These options allow you to make tax-deductible contributions that you can invest in vehicles such as stocks, bonds, mutual funds, and CDs. In these plans, the funds' earnings compound tax deferred.

All the money you stash in a self-employment retirement plan must be self-employment income. That means income from freelance writing, consulting, arts and crafts, or any other way you earn money on your own. Farmers, doctors, lawyers, and other professionals who are not covered by corporate plans may also fund a self-employment plan. Some of these plans require you to contribute a certain amount of money every year. Other plans allow you to contribute whatever you please, up to an annual maximum, or nothing at all if you can't afford it or if you produce no self-employment income for that year. Like other retirement plans, you pay a 10 percent penalty and income taxes if you withdraw funds from a self-employment retirement plan before age 59½. For more information on these plans, see the Resources listed in Appendix B.

Individual Retirement Accounts (IRAs)

Even if you or your spouse have a defined benefit or defined contribution plan through your employers, or a Keogh or SEP if one or both of you are self-employed, you can also establish an IRA as a tax-sheltered vehicle to save for retirement. It can be quite complex to determine whether or not you qualify for a deduction for your IRA contribution. But in any case, the funds inside the IRA grow tax deferred, and in the case of a Roth IRA, tax free!

Many people who formerly contributed to IRAs do not do so any longer because of the complexities of the law, and the possibility that they will not be able to deduct their contributions. That may be a big mistake, particularly because of the attractiveness of Roth IRAs. Funding your IRA must be accomplished totally on your own initiative because no employer will offer you one. But this flexible type of account, which you can manage however you want and which offers an enormous range of investment options, is worth the extra effort.

Under the current rules for a traditional IRA, you and your spouse may be eligible to set aside $4,000 or more for each of you if under age 50. The type of IRA account that is most appropriate for you (and allowed by Uncle Sam) depends on your income level, age, and other retirement plans. Keep in mind that an IRA is not an investment; it's a legal structure that allows you to invest in traditional investments such as mutual funds or individual securities.

Deductible and Nondeductible Traditional IRAs

Depending on your employment status and level of income, the contribution you make to an IRA may or may not be deductible. If you are not eligible to participate in any qualified retirement plan that includes the defined benefit and defined contribution plans discussed above, your IRA contribution of up to $4,000 a year and $4,000 for a nonworking spouse are tax deductible, no matter what your income so long as you have earned income for this amount or more. That amounts to about a $1,100 tax savings for each $4,000 contribution if you are in the 28 percent federal tax bracket. Congress has raised contribution limits from $4,000 in 2005 if under age 50 to $6,000 by 2008 for those age 50 and older. The limit for younger folks caps at $5,000 per year in 2008. Because the limits keep changing, consult your accountant or check with the IRS each year.

Although a nondeductible IRA is not as lucrative up front as a deductible IRA, the nondeductible form can still be a potent long-term tax shelter for accumulating a retirement nest egg. Because all dividends and capital gains are tax deferred until you are at least age 59½, you gain the advantage of tax-free compounding. In the long run, that shelter can be worth far more than the one-time tax reduction resulting from a deductible IRA contribution.

You can open an IRA account until the April 15 tax deadline and, if you are eligible, deduct your contribution on the previous year's tax return. However, don't wait until the last minute to invest your money because you lose valuable time for your earnings to compound tax deferred. It is far better to make your IRA deposit soon after January 1 of the year you will claim the deduction. This way, you have the full year to take advantage of the tax shelter. For example, it would generally be better to contribute $2,000 on January 3, 2006, for the 2006 tax year than to wait until April 15, 2007, because you will gain more than 15 months of additional tax-deferred compounding. You can continue to contribute to your traditional IRA until you reach age 70½, at which point you must start withdrawing capital according to an IRS schedule.

Roth IRAs

In addition to traditional IRAs, which permit your investments to compound tax deferred, the Taxpayer Relief Act of 1997 created the Roth IRA. The Roth IRA allows your capital to accumulate tax free if you follow certain rules. It is named after Delaware senator William V. Roth Jr., who championed the idea of expanded IRAs.

You and your spouse can each invest up to $4,000 a year if under age 50 in a Roth IRA, even after you reach age 70½. You can withdraw all the principal and earnings totally tax free after age 59½, as long as the assets have remained in the IRA for at least five years after you made the first contribution. The assets also can be withdrawn tax free if you are hit by a major disability. If you die before you start withdrawing from a Roth, the proceeds go to your beneficiaries tax free. Unlike regular IRAs, you do not have to take distributions from a Roth IRA starting at age 70½. In fact, you don't have to take distributions at all in your lifetime. If you prefer, you may pass the assets in the Roth to your beneficiaries free of income taxes.

You do not receive a deduction for contributing to a Roth IRA unlike some other kinds of IRAs. But the value of tax-free withdrawals should far exceed the tax break from the deduction.

There are, of course, income limitations on who can open Roth IRAs. Each spouse can contribute the full $4,000 if you are a married couple with an adjusted gross income of $150,000 or less or a single person with an adjusted gross income of $95,000 or less. The amount you can contribute becomes lower for income between $150,000 and $160,000 for couples filing jointly and between $95,000 and $110,000 for singles. If your income is over these limits, you are not allowed to make a Roth contribution.

You can roll over assets from a traditional IRA to a Roth IRA under certain circumstances. If your adjusted gross income is $100,000 or less, you can roll over existing nondeductible and deductible IRA balances into a Roth without owing the 10 percent prepayment penalty. However, when you undertake such a rollover, you must pay income tax on all previously untaxed contributions and earnings. So before you initiate this transaction, figure out where you will get the money to pay this potentially large tax bill!

Whether it makes sense to roll over money into a Roth from a traditional IRA depends on several factors. In general, the more you have accumulated in a traditional IRA, the more tax you will pay when you roll over to a Roth, and the more time you will need to recover those taxes from tax-free withdrawals.

If you are young and have not accumulated very much in a traditional IRA, it might make more sense to roll over your balances to a Roth than if you have amassed a large sum that would generate a huge tax when rolled over. But, remember you can convert just a portion each year to spread out the tax hit over several years. Many mutual fund and brokerage firms, including Fidelity, T. Rowe Price, Vanguard, and Merrill Lynch, offer their customers free or low-cost software programs and information on their Web sites that will help you figure out whether a rollover to a Roth makes sense in your situation. The best way to take advantage of the Roth is to set one up when you are in your twenties, contribute the maximum allowed every year, invest the money for maximum capital gains, and withdraw huge sums totally free of taxes as needed in retirement.

How to Invest Your IRA Funds

When you understand the rules of IRA contributions and withdrawals, learn to maximize your investment options. IRAs offer many investment vehicles, including individual stocks; bonds; mutual funds; unit investment trusts (UITs); limited partnerships; commodities funds; CDs; options; and gold, silver, platinum, and palladium coins minted by the U.S. government, such as the American Eagle gold and platinum coins. The two classes of investments in which you cannot legally deposit IRA funds are collectibles and physical real estate (both your home and rental real estate investments—real estate investment trusts, or REITS, are different). The term *collectibles* is defined as artwork, stamps, numismatic coins, gems, antiques, and gold and silver coins minted outside the United States.

Although it is legal to invest in municipal bonds as part of an IRA, it doesn't make sense to do so because you don't need tax-exempt income in a tax-sheltered account. Two philosophies exist regarding the best way to take advantage of the tax-deferred feature of IRAs. Some investment advisors favor growth and maintain that you want the fastest growing investments possible, such as aggressive growth stocks or stock funds, because an IRA is a long-term vehicle that allows you to accumulate significant amounts of assets by retirement. You can trade in and out of stocks, bonds, and options without caring about the tax consequences of your actions because all gains are tax deferred for years.

Other investment advisors believe that you should stuff your IRA with the highest yielding investments available, such as high-yield stocks, bonds, mortgage-backed securities, income mutual funds, CDs, and UITs. They reason that because all IRA income compounds tax deferred, it's to your advantage to earn the highest income possible. Therefore, if interest rates are high, probably the best IRA investment is a zero-coupon bond, which automatically locks in a high rate of interest reinvestment until the bond matures. With this type of bond you also know exactly how much capital you will have accumulated as many as 20 years in the future. No other investment guarantees that.

Both ways of thinking about IRA investments are valid. You can decide to try one strategy or the other, or you can mix the two. However you allocate your IRA funds, integrate your IRA into your total investment portfolio to achieve a proper balance. For instance, if your employer's salary reduction plan is invested in conservative GICs or bonds, sink your IRA funds in more aggressive growth stock funds. On the other hand, if you own many growth stocks in your personal portfolio, as well as growth mutual funds in your 401(k), be more conservative with your IRA money, and select high-quality bonds or bond funds.

However you allocate the money, it is more important to open an IRA early in your working life and contribute to it year after year. The capital that accumulates in your IRA could make the difference between a comfortable and a meager retirement.

Planning Ahead: Adding Other Savings and Investments to Your Retirement Fund

In addition to what you might receive from Social Security, pensions, or IRAs, the capital you accumulate through your regular savings and investment program will provide the majority of most people's retirement income. As a general rule, try to save as much as you can as early in your career as possible for maximum growth. Aim to save a minimum of 10 percent of your gross income each year, allocated among salary reduction plans, IRAs, and Keoghs, as well as your independent savings accounts and investments.

Ideally, you should invest most of your capital for growth opportunities while you are in your twenties, thirties, and forties to accumulate the largest pool of capital possible. This means buying growth stocks, aggressive growth mutual funds, junk bonds, and international investments. As you move into your forties and mid-fifties, scale back the risk level of your investments, and purchase equity income funds, convertibles securities, balanced funds, and other vehicles that offer income as well as growth.

By the time you retire, if you have accumulated a substantial amount of capital, you can become even more conservative and invest 40 to 60 percent or more of your money in low-growth vehicles, such as government and municipal bonds, CDs, money market funds, and Treasury bills that will produce regular income that you can live on. However, don't sink all of your money in totally safe investments once you retire: You'll probably live many years after retirement, and to keep up with inflation, you'll need the continuous growth of capital that equities can provide. Fortunately, that's a long way off, so let's get back to some of the issues facing you now, such as deciding how you want to invest your money.

▶ Adventurer or Armchair Traveler: What's Your Investment Risk Tolerance?

By now, you've probably realized that you and your spouse will have to take some calculated risks to attain your financial goals, but this doesn't mean you'll necessarily be comfortable doing it. The quiz in Roadmap 4.2 will give you and your spouse some insight into the level of risk you each feel able to take. It's best to take the quiz separately and then get together to compare the results. Answer each of the questions, giving yourself one point for answer one, two points for answer two, and up to four points for answer four. Then add up the points to see what kind of a risk taker you are. Then, you and your spouse must come to an agreement on your risk tolerance as a couple.

Keep your risk score in mind as you read the rest of the book. If you tend toward the conservative, you should resist the temptation to put a lot of money in riskier investments even though they may sound promising. At the same time, remember that you don't want to have all your assets in only the safest places.

If you are a moderate-risk investor, put more of your money in less secure sectors as long as you carefully gauge the level of risk you are taking. For high-risk investors, allocate more of your money to more aggressive investments, but don't neglect putting some portion of your assets in safer instruments.

Risk Tolerance Quiz

A. If someone made me an offer to invest 15 percent of my net worth in a deal that he said had an 80 percent chance of being profitable, the amount of profit would have to be:

1. No amount of profit would be worth that kind of risk.

2. Seven times the amount I invested.

3. Three times the amount I invested.

4. At least as much as I invested in the first place.

Points: _____

B. How comfortable would I be assuming a $10,000 debt in the hope of achieving a $20,000 gain over the next few months?

1. Totally uncomfortable—I would never do it.

2. Somewhat uncomfortable—I would probably never do it.

3. Somewhat comfortable—I might do it.

4. Very comfortable—I would jump at the chance to do it.

Points: _____

C. I am holding a lottery ticket that has gotten me to the finals, and I have a one-in-four chance of winning a $100,000 prize. The least I would be willing to sell my ticket for before the drawing is:

1. $15,000.

2. $20,000.

3. $35,000.

4. $60,000.

Points: _____

D. I have spent more than $150 on one or more of these activities in the past: professional sports gambling, recreational betting on poker or basketball games that I participate in, and casino gambling.

1. I have never participated in any of these activities.

2. I have participated in these activities only a few times in my life.

3. I have participated in one of these activities in the past year.

4. I have participated in two or more of these activities in the past year.

Points: _____

E. Whenever I have to decide where to invest a large amount of money, I:

1. delay the decision.
2. get somebody else (like my family members or friends) to decide for me.
3. share the decision with advisors.
4. decide on my own.

Points: _____

F. If a stock I bought doubled in the year after I bought it, I would:

1. sell all my shares.
2. sell half of my shares.
3. not sell any shares.
4. buy more shares.

Points: _____

G. Which of the following describes how I make my investment decisions?

1. Never on my own
2. Sometimes on my own
3. Often on my own
4. Always on my own

Points: _____

H. My luck in investing is:

1. terrible.
2. average.
3. better than average.
4. fantastic.

Points: _____

I. My investments are successful mainly because:

1. God is always on my side.
2. I was in the right place at the right time.
3. when opportunities arose, I took advantage of them.
4. I carefully planned them to work out that way.

Points: _____

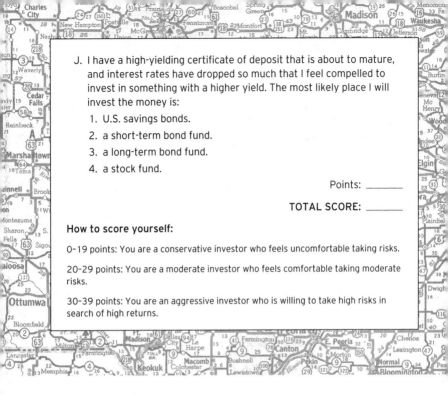

J. I have a high-yielding certificate of deposit that is about to mature, and interest rates have dropped so much that I feel compelled to invest in something with a higher yield. The most likely place I will invest the money is:

1. U.S. savings bonds.
2. a short-term bond fund.
3. a long-term bond fund.
4. a stock fund.

Points: _____

TOTAL SCORE: _____

How to score yourself:

0–19 points: You are a conservative investor who feels uncomfortable taking risks.

20–29 points: You are a moderate investor who feels comfortable taking moderate risks.

30–39 points: You are an aggressive investor who is willing to take high risks in search of high returns.

Be cautious about becoming so enthusiastic about an investing idea that you put a large amount of your capital in an investment that goes bust.

Wherever you stand on the risk spectrum, keep in mind that dealing with your personal finances, in general, and investing, in particular, is not only about maximizing the amount of dollars in your pocket. Finding your financial comfort zone is also important, so that you feel emotionally secure about the decisions you are making. It's no use becoming rich if you die from the stress of attaining your wealth, even though your heirs might disagree!

Plan Your Route: Determine Your Investment Parameters

No one knows your investment profile better than you do. Do you want low-risk, medium-risk, or high-risk investments? What type of assets do you want to hold: long-term or short-term? Keep the answers to these questions in mind as you establish your investment strategy.

Risk is an unusual concept. It is the hinge that drives most investment decisions. Will you put your money in the stock market, or will you sleep better at night with all of your money in the bank? Make these decisions together.

Risk is the one ingredient that makes determining your investment parameters so fascinating. We all understand that risk is what gives investors the potential for higher returns. The skill lies in creating a blend of investments that will allow you to achieve the maximum overall rate of return on your portfolio without exposing yourself to unnecessary risks.

Establish Your Time Span. What is your time span for reaching your goals? Do you have 40 years to save or only five years? It is very important that you plan for the appropriate time horizon. To do this, you'll want to develop a timeline for your financial plan. Again, this timeline needs to be fairly specific and should include all your short- and long-term goals and dreams. Your timeline will be as individual as you both are, and it must include the specific amounts of money that you expect you both will need to accomplish each goal.

Develop Your Monthly Investing Strategy. Few newlyweds can afford to give their financial advisor a $50,000 lump sum to invest in a tax-deferred vehicle for 25 years with an average 8 percent rate of return, but if they could, it might be a good thing. Unfortunately, it only works if you have an extra $50,000 lying around. If you are like most people, a monthly investment strategy is more realistic and will help you accomplish the same goal.

A $360.05 monthly investment, earning the same 8 percent return in some type of tax-deferred vehicle, will grow to $342,423.75 in 25 years. But what if you don't have $360.05 to invest each month? It will take five additional years if you invest $229.76 at 8 percent to acquire the same amount. Or, if you and your spouse are not risk averse, you could invest in more aggressive vehicles and hope to make a 10 percent return over a 25-year period. If you use this strategy, a $258.08 monthly savings will accomplish the same goal.

You must begin to save for your future. Some people are amazed at the actual amount of money required to fund their future financial goals, yet they don't hesitate to take on a huge monthly mortgage or a large seven-year car payment. Many people can't imagine saving $200, $300, or $500 a month to meet their future obligations.

It all comes back to your choices. How are you going to spend your money now? These numbers reinforce the Social Security Administration's contention that only 2 to 3 percent of the U.S. population (approximately) can afford to retire at age 65 without any additional outside assistance.

The choice is yours. Pay yourself first and plan to invest at least 10 percent of every paycheck. No doubt this strategy may mean making some changes in the way you currently spend your income. But the question remains: Do you want to be in the 3 percent or the 97 percent category?

▶ Traveling with Kids: Saving for Retirement vs. Saving for College Educations

If you're about to get married or newly married you probably don't have children yet, unless this is the second time around. Some may think, "Why talk about retirement now when I'll probably be saving to put the kids through school way before I'll be able to save for retirement?" If you have to choose between the two, and many of us do, a better strategy is to save for retirement rather than fund your children's education. (We'll talk more about saving and other options for college education in chapter 6.)

This plan is not to suggest that paying for college is a less important goal. In fact, for some people, paying for a college education might be their highest priority. But, as an investment strategy, it makes sense to focus on your potential retirement needs first. Take full advantage of tax-deferred retirement accounts. Then make additional investments that are earmarked for college, and you have the best chance to achieve both of your goals.

There are many ways to pay for the cost of a college education when the time comes, but if you haven't saved and invested properly for retirement, you will be out of luck. Here's why.

Once again, to meet your retirement goals, it's important to start saving early and utilize tax-deferred, employer-provided programs if available, such as 401(k) and 403(b) plans. As mentioned earlier in this chapter, these plans, in addition to saving on a pretax basis (the equivalent of a tax deduction), provide the benefit of tax-deferred compounding. Employer plans also give you a convenient and disciplined means to invest on a regular basis and benefit from "dollar cost averaging" through up and down markets. (Dollar cost averaging refers to the practice of investing the same number of dollars regularly. When prices are high, you get fewer shares; when prices are low you get more shares. Over time, you wind up with more shares bought at a low price and fewer bought at a high price, and your average price is a good one.) Because of the "use it or lose it" nature of these accounts as well as IRAs and Roth IRAs, maximizing your annual contributions makes sense.

In some cases, retirement accounts can be used for both retirement and college. For example, withdrawals from Roth IRAs can be used without penalty for some qualified educational expenses, and loans can be taken from 401(k) accounts. For couples having children later in life, the need for college money may coincide with the start of retirement. In this case funds can be withdrawn from retirement accounts without penalty.

Hit the Road! What to Do *Now*

Even if you're a risk-averse investor who wants to make the most prudent investments, don't be so cautious that you don't do anything. The following list of steps will help you and your spouse get on track for a more secure financial future.

Maximize Retirement Plan Contributions. One of the best ways to save for retirement is to take advantage of your retirement plan at work. A 401(k) allows you to invest money directly from your paycheck, before taxes are taken out. In addition, many companies will match a percentage of the employee's contributions. Think of the company match as a tax-free bonus from your employer. But you must participate in the plan to get the bonus. Money in a qualified retirement account grows tax deferred until you begin to withdraw it during retirement. Self-employed individuals may open a *SIMPLE IRA* or SEP retirement plan.

Fund Your IRAs No Matter What. Even if you're covered by another retirement plan, contribute to an IRA. If you meet eligibility requirements, a Roth IRA is generally the best option. Traditional IRA contributions may or may not be tax deductible, depending on your income and whether you or your spouse is covered by another qualified plan. Even if your contribution is not deductible, IRAs are a great way to invest for your future because your money grows and compounds tax deferred. The use it or lose it nature of these accounts is another reason to maximize contributions annually. Retirement accounts, including 401(k)s and all varieties of IRAs, have annual limits. If contributions are not made during the tax year, the opportunity is lost forever.

Invest to Meet Long-Term Goals. If you're a late starter, balance risk with potential return. You do not want to jeopardize your financial future by investing too aggressively, but investing too conservatively is risky, too. Although it may be hard to think about investing in growth-oriented investments in difficult times, remember that over the long term, these investments historically have outpaced more secure investments. As you get closer to retirement, adjust the allocation of your assets toward more conservative investments. Even if you feel confident making your own portfolio allocation decisions, consider obtaining a qualified financial planner's advice on portfolio design and asset allocation.

Fund Your Retirement Needs First. Make saving for retirement a priority over putting away money for your children's college education. If you don't have enough money to cover tuition bills, your children can apply for financial aid or student loans. That's not an option when it comes to funding retirement. Make sure that you're saving all you can or need for retirement before you earmark substantial funds for the kids' college programs.

Spend Less and Save More. Track how you spend your money. Evaluate your spending habits, and cut back on nonessentials. For example, cutting out that morning cafe latte saves a couple of dollars each day. It may not sound like much, but $2 invested daily for 20 years at 8 percent interest adds up to more than $36,000. A number of small changes like that can save you big bucks. Determine where you can make cuts, and redirect your savings to your retirement accounts. Pay yourself first: Arrange to have a fixed amount transferred each month to your mutual fund or IRA.

Consider the New Retirement Mentality. Read the book *The New Retirementality,* by Mitch Anthony, published by Dearborn Trade. In this book, Anthony explores the significant myths and realities of retirement. The American Association of Retired Persons (AARP) (http://www.aarp.org) has a wealth of information on financial and lifestyle issues.

Work Longer. We are living longer. To fund that length of retirement, it will take a very big nest egg. Consider working longer—either in a full- or part-time capacity—to help manage the requirements for saving more.

Take One Step at a Time. Don't be overwhelmed by what you need to save. Focus on cutting expenses and diverting your savings to retirement savings.

Make securing a comfortable retirement a conscious choice. Work toward it daily, weekly, and monthly.

Get Professional Help. Seeking help now is especially important because declines in the stock market have decimated the savings of many people and low interest rates have hurt retirees living on fixed incomes. Many Americans feel that they have nowhere to go for independent, objective advice, but a new breed of financial planner has emerged during the past few years who specifically serves middle-income Americans. These planners do not accept commissions or require long-term contracts. They charge by the hour and are happy to provide as little or as much help as their clients need. To learn about the nation's largest group of fee-only financial planners (as opposed to planners who earn commissions on what they sell) and read related articles by *Wall Street Journal* columnist Jonathan Clements, visit http//:http://www. garrettplanningnetwork.com.

Learn All You Can. Some additional sources of good information include the following:

► Financial Planning Association (http://www.fpanet.org)
► National Association of Personal Financial Planners (http://www.napfa. org)
► National Retirement Planning Coalition (http://www.retireonyourterms. org)
► Bloomberg News (http://www.bloomberg.com).
► Garrett Planning Network (http://www.garrettplanningnetwork.com).

The End of the Journey

Estate Planning and Making a Will

When you're just getting married, maybe the last thing on your mind is what will happen to your assets when you die. But because you're also thinking about how your finances will change when you marry, no financial plan is complete without a detailed discussion of estate planning and the making of a will. This chapter covers both these topics as well as how to protect your assets (which is, after all, the goal of estate planning) by setting up a trust. In addition, special situations are explained, such as how to protect the inheritance of your children from a previous marriage.

▶ Plan Your Journey Well: Show You Care About Your Heirs

Most people put more time and effort into planning their summer vacations than into thinking about how they are going to take care of their families after they die. Is that the message you want to pass on to your family, that a vacation was worth more of your attention than planning for them in their time of need?

If you are about to be or are newly married you should consider preparing an estate plan. You don't need to be rich to need an estate plan. The purpose of an estate plan is to ensure that you can pass on the messages you want to the people you care about, according to the conditions that you dictate.

When you hear the word "estate," you may envision something big, grand, and far beyond your own financial reality, such as a mansion, for example. However, in the eyes of the law, your estate is simply everything you own, by yourself and with others. Your home, car, furniture, bank accounts, jewelry, life insurance policy, retirement plan, stocks and bonds, and other assets are all part of your estate. Although some people have large estates worth millions, the estates of most Americans are relatively modest.

Look Ahead, Down the Road: Estate Plans Let *You* Decide Where Your Assets Go

Although thinking about death may make you uncomfortable, you will die someday. When that unfortunate event occurs, whether it be tomorrow or decades from now, your assets will be distributed, and your estate may have to pay estate taxes. What you should decide now is whether you want to control how your estate is settled or whether you want to leave it up to the probate court, which might distribute your property in a manner that would not please you if you were alive.

If you ignore the rather daunting process of estate planning, you not only lose control of how your worldly possessions will be handed out, but your estate might pay thousands of dollars in estate taxes, which could have been easily avoided. Current federal estate tax rates start at 41 percent on transfers in excess of $2 million and can be as high as 50 percent on transfers in excess of $2.5 million. And some states also tack on inheritance taxes (to non-spouses only).

Fewer than 70 percent of Americans have a will or any type of document that will help them distribute their assets after they die. If you make the effort to maximize basic estate-planning techniques, however, your spouse, children, grandchildren, and others for whom you care deeply will receive a far greater inheritance to enrich their lives. Therefore, even though you won't benefit personally after your death (It's true, you can't take it with you!), you will live with the satisfaction of knowing that you have done all you can to pass on the fruits of your life's labor to your loved ones.

Many people never plan their estates because they are intimidated by the subject, they think they have nothing of value to pass on, or they are concerned about the fees lawyers charge to draw up wills and other estate-planning documents. It may also be true that these people never think about the subject at all and go through life assuming that their estates will somehow take care of themselves when they die.

Americans who do no estate planning might be shocked to learn that when people die without wills (or, as lawyers put it, *intestate*), the probate court takes over and can dominate their survivors' lives for years. It is not a simple process. After all, estate planning settles not only the disposition of possessions and money but also other major life decisions, including custody of children, if you decide to have them. If you never express your preferences before you die, a judge who probably never met you must determine what's best for your family. The small amount of time and money you invest now to dictate what happens when you die is well worth the effort. Most of all, planning your estate gives you the peace of mind that your affairs will be handled properly and according to your wishes when you die.

A Multiple-Lane Highway: What Estate Planning Entails

The term *estate planning* is mysterious to many people, but essentially the process is intended to help you answer nine critical questions and then implement your decisions.

1. Who will inherit your remaining money and possessions after the costs of settling your estate are subtracted?
2. How can you prepare a strategy to give away many of your assets as tax-free gifts while you are alive to minimize the assets that will be depleted by estate taxes when you die?
3. If both of you die while your children are still young, who should be guardian for your children while they are younger than age 18? (This guardian, who may be an individual or a couple, would take your children into their home and raise them, so you must feel as certain as possible that they would bring up your children in a manner of which you would approve.)
4. Who should be trustee to administer any trusts you may establish?
5. Whom should you nominate as an executor of your estate; that is, an independent person you trust who will faithfully carry out the provisions of your will? This is often a lawyer familiar with your family.
6. What should be done with your body after you die? You may want it donated for medical research or cremated, for instance. You may also

want to specify how and where you want to be buried. Some people also set a limit on the amount they want spent on their funerals.

7. What must you do to appoint a successor custodian for the assets of a child or grandchild, if you currently act as a custodian for a Uniform Gifts to Minors Act account? (If you don't specify the successor custodian, a court will decide for you.)

8. How should you plan to make gifts of either money or property to your favorite charity, university, church, or synagogue? (Without your specific written instructions, no such gifts can be authorized by the executor of your estate.)

9. What should you do to prepare for the time you may be unable to care for yourself? You can prepare what are called *advance directives* that give instructions on the kinds of health care you want provided or withheld in the event you cannot communicate your wishes. In some states, you can specify in a *living will*, for instance, whether you want extraordinary treatment to keep you alive if you go into a coma. You can also appoint someone you trust as a *health care power of attorney* to make difficult decisions about your medical treatment if you are unable to make these decisions yourself.

If you don't make all of these crucial decisions before you die, they will be settled for you, often by people you don't know, in ways you may not approve of. So be sure you and your spouse have very clear understandings of how you each want to be cared for. By taking care of these decisions in a calm, unhurried way far in advance of your death, you avoid any need for a hastily drawn document or, even worse, a *deathbed will,* which most likely will be contested later. Clearly, it is far better to determine how you want your estate handled long before the inevitable day comes when such decisions must be made.

The Wrong Road: What Happens If You Don't Have an Estate Plan

As mentioned earlier, fewer than 70 percent of Americans have a will or any type of document that will aid them in the disposal of their assets after they die. If you don't have an estate plan, the consequences can be severe for you, your assets, and your surviving family members.

Your state of residence decides who makes your medical decisions for you in the event you are unable to do so. Most people think of estate plans as documents that determine what happens after death. Actually, some of the most important estate planning dictates what happens while you are still alive. Health care directives, living wills, health care proxies, or durable powers of attorney for health care all allow you to name someone who can make medical decisions for you in the event you are unable. The power of attorney for asset management allows you to name someone who can sign your name to financial documents. Living trusts can state the manner in which you want your finances handled, how distributions should be made to you and your family if you are no longer in a position to make those types of decisions, and who will be responsible for your affairs under certain circumstances.

The state decides who inherits your assets. The state could decide to give your assets to your spouse, your children, your parents, your siblings, or some more distant relative, depending on your circumstances. In some states, dying without a will results in most of your assets going to your children, with only a small remainder left for your surviving spouse. It's possible that you and the state may think alike when it comes to naming your beneficiaries, but what are the chances of that? The rules are the same for every person in the state. Look at your neighbors next door, across the street, and around the corner. What is the likelihood that you all will have the same opinions on who should inherit your assets at death?

The state decides the conditions in which your beneficiaries inherit your assets. For young children, it is possible that a court would order the assets to stay in a trust until they are age 18 or maybe 21. Yet many children may not use this money wisely at either of these ages. Perhaps they would be more likely to buy (and wreck) a Porsche than do something responsible, such as fund their education, buy a home, or save for their retirement. So if you're not willing to give your children all your money at age 18 or 21 while you're still alive, why would you let someone else do it when you die and are no longer there to give them guidance?

The state decides who takes care of your children. If you have not appointed a guardian and a trustee for your minor children, the state will appoint them for you after your death if you and your spouse both die before your children turn 18. It may, or may not be the people whom you would have chosen to raise your children and oversee their assets.

The state can sell you assets to pay your estate taxes. If your estate is illiquid (not easily convertible to cash), and you have not planned for estate tax payment, valuable assets may have to be sold to pay estate taxes. This may mean selling the family farm or business that you wanted your spouse to keep. It may mean having to sell securities or real estate when the market is down. And it might mean selling your surviving spouse's home.

The estate tax, inheritance tax, and transfer costs can take more than 40 percent of your hard-earned estate away before it goes to your heirs. Planning in advance can significantly increase the amount going to the people and charities you care about.

► Watch Those Tolls: What You Need to Know About Estate Taxes

When you die, your estate may have to pay taxes. The more taxes it must pay, the less will be left to be distributed to your beneficiaries. Therefore, for those with substantial estates, tax minimization is an important part of estate planning. Depending on your state, taxes may be an issue even if your estate is not worth a lot. The following paragraphs describe some of the taxes your estate may have to pay.

Estate Income Tax. Your estate must pay this tax if the income it earns in any tax year exceeds the standard exemptions an estate receives.

Personal Income Tax. This is the tax due on your income earned in the year of your death.

Federal Estate Tax. Your estate must pay this tax only if its value exceeds a certain dollar amount. The amount is based on the current market value of all the assets in your estate, not just those that go through probate. The amount is known as the *unified tax credit*. In 2006, the amount of this tax credit was $2,000,000. Therefore, if your estate is worth $2.5 million at the time of your death in 2006, $500,000 of your estate would be subject to federal estate taxes.

A law was passed in 2001 that authorized gradual increases in the size of the unified tax credit and an end to the federal estate tax, though only for one year. After that year ends, the federal estate tax will be reinstated, but there are questions regarding the size of the unified tax credit at that point. Therefore, check with an estate planning attorney for the most up-to-date information, especially because at the time of this writing there is talk that the new estate tax law may be repealed or changed. The increases

Tollbooth 5.1

How the Unified Tax Credit Is Increasing

2006	$2,000,000	2009	$3,500,000
2007	$2,000,000	2010	No federal estate tax
2008	$2,000,000	2011	$1,000,000*

*unless the law is changed

in the unified tax credit stop in 2009. Tollbooth 5.1 shows its amounts for the years 2006–2011.

State Estate Tax. A few states have their own estate taxes, although these states are becoming fewer and fewer in number. Although they may tax estates valued at less than the federal estate tax threshold, potentially affecting more modest estates, the good news is that their tax rates are considerably lower than the federal government's.

The Inheritance Tax. Some states tax the inheritance that a non-spouse beneficiary may receive. The tax is levied against the value of the inheritance, but a trend is growing among the states to eliminate this tax. At the time this book was written, less than one-fourth of the states still had this tax.

The taxes your estate owes must be paid before your beneficiaries can receive the assets that you have left them. If you made special provisions in your will for paying your taxes, your executor will follow them. Otherwise, your executor will use the money in your residuary estate to pay your taxes.

If your residuary estate does not have enough money to pay all of the taxes your estate owes, payment of those taxes will be apportioned among all of the assets in your estate, starting with general bequests and then moving to specific bequests. Personal property will be tapped before real property. As a result, your beneficiaries may end up with less than what you had intended them to receive. Unless all estate-related taxes are paid to the IRS, the agency will use any of the means available to it to collect taxes, including seizing assets and levying bank accounts.

▶ Look in Your Rearview Mirror: If You've Been Married Before

Financial planning for a second marriage is more complex than the first time you were married, particularly if you have more money saved, if either of you has debts or less than perfect credit, or if you have children from a previous relationship and new family members who may have competing interests in your property. Consider taking the following steps to prevent potential conflicts and ensure that your future financial picture stays healthy.

Consider a Prenuptial Agreement. As mentioned in Chapter 1, prenuptial agreements can be a healthy result of an honest conversation about finances. A prenuptial is a good idea if you have substantial assets or children to protect because it spells out the rights, obligations, and duties that each of you will have during the marriage. The goal is to identify the assets and liabilities each partner brings to the marriage and determine how these assets and those acquired during the marriage will be divided, if necessary. This planning can help avoid misunderstandings as well as severe problems should the unthinkable happen.

Review How Your Assets Are Titled. For you and your new spouse, any property you acquire after getting married can be owned as *joint tenants with right of survivorship.* (More on this later in the chapter.) This designation allows property to pass directly to the surviving spouse should one of you die. Both of you should also check your current life insurance policies and retirement accounts, such as all 401(k)s and IRAs, to update your choice of beneficiaries. If you want to name someone other than your new spouse as the primary beneficiary of your qualified retirement plan assets, you need your spouse's written permission to do so.

Update Your Wills and Trusts. Be sure to update your will so it clearly spells out your goals. It is also a good idea to make sure that everyone concerned knows your wishes. If your children feel slighted, they might challenge your will after your death. Also, if you have stepchildren to whom you want to leave part of your estate, use your will to spell out your wishes for them. Trusts can be useful in dictating the way you want your assets disposed (as we'll see, in the section on trusts later in this chapter). You can attach strings to how your money will be used and managed. For example, you might want

Dear Lynn,

Thanks so much for your support during Bruce's funeral. I still can't believe my husband is dead, but I have to pull myself together because I have so many financial problems and decisions to face.

Bruce didn't prepare a will or estate plans: He always said I was being silly when I asked him to because we're both so young. He was healthy, but he worked in construction, so there was always a high chance of an accident, which is exactly what happened.

Now Bruce's ex-wife is demanding to know the provisions Bruce has made for their daughter. I've told her he made no arrangements, but she accused me of lying. She said she'll make sure they receive a fair share of Bruce's estate, and she's suing us! What estate? We have a nice home and a few dollars in the bank, but that's it. His $50,000 life insurance policy will just barely pay off the mortgage and the burial expenses. How can I prove that someone, who by all other indications was a great dad, didn't make provisions for his child in the event of his death? Now what do I do?

—Janine

a trust to make sure that your spouse can live in your home as long as he or she wants and that your children will eventually inherit it.

Consider Your Children's Needs and Your New Spouse's Needs. When you marry, most of your assets typically pass to your spouse when you die. In a traditional family, that's not a problem, and the family assets typically pass to the children after both parents are gone. With your remarriage, however, you will probably want to provide for your spouse and any children of this marriage, as well as your children from your previous marriage. Now is the time to take proactive steps to avoid a yours, mine, and ours dispute.

Some potential problems include the following:

▶ When you're dead and your spouse has retired, he or she may want safer, income-producing investments. Your children, however, may want a more aggressive growth strategy so that something will be left for them when they inherit.

▶ Your children may watch every penny that your spouse spends. How will they feel if your surviving spouse wants to buy a new car?

▶ If your new spouse is much younger than you, your children may have to wait a long time before they inherit what remains of your estate.

Here are some possible solutions:

1. Put together a plan that effectively disconnects the money left for your spouse from the money to be left to your children. You will, of course, want to consult an attorney or estate planning professional to ensure that your plan is structured properly.

2. Life insurance can be an effective way of making sure that your children receive money when you die instead of having to wait until both you and your spouse have passed away. Your children can be the primary beneficiaries of your life insurance policies. Another option is to have your children take out a life policy on you that makes them the owners and beneficiaries of the policy and you the insured. You can gift them money each year, which they can use to pay the premiums. Or you can establish an irrevocable trust to hold the life insurance for their benefit. The latter approach can work well if you currently have minor children.

▶ Before You Write Your Itinerary: Determine What Assets You Own

Creating an inventory of your assets and debts is an essential first step when you are preparing to write your will. Among other things, the inventory information is essential to assess the value of your estate, determine whether estate taxes are an issue for you, and help you evaluate whether you should use other estate planning tools besides a will. Creating an inventory also helps minimize the possibility that you will overlook some of your assets when you are doing your estate planning.

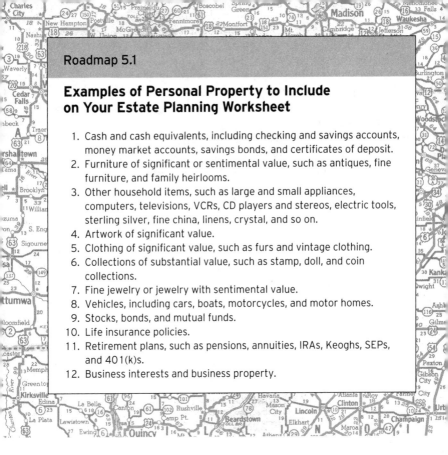

Roadmap 5.1

Examples of Personal Property to Include on Your Estate Planning Worksheet

1. Cash and cash equivalents, including checking and savings accounts, money market accounts, savings bonds, and certificates of deposit.
2. Furniture of significant or sentimental value, such as antiques, fine furniture, and family heirlooms.
3. Other household items, such as large and small appliances, computers, televisions, VCRs, CD players and stereos, electric tools, sterling silver, fine china, linens, crystal, and so on.
4. Artwork of significant value.
5. Clothing of significant value, such as furs and vintage clothing.
6. Collections of substantial value, such as stamp, doll, and coin collections.
7. Fine jewelry or jewelry with sentimental value.
8. Vehicles, including cars, boats, motorcycles, and motor homes.
9. Stocks, bonds, and mutual funds.
10. Life insurance policies.
11. Retirement plans, such as pensions, annuities, IRAs, Keoghs, SEPs, and 401(k)s.
12. Business interests and business property.

Roadmap 5.1 provides examples of the kinds of personal property you may need to list on your asset inventory worksheet. Tollbooth 5.2 is the actual worksheet. (Ask your attorney for help if you have trouble completing the worksheet.) You will notice that the worksheet has spaces for listing and describing each of your assets, for indicating how you own each asset, for noting the percentage of each asset you own, and for recording each asset's estimated net value. Recording this information tells you four things:

1. Which assets you can give away to your beneficiaries
2. Which assets will go through probate
3. Whether you should be concerned about minimizing the number of assets that will go through probate (more about probate later in this chapter)

Tollbooth 5.2

Your Estate Planning Worksheet

ASSET INVENTORY

Description of Asset	Type of Ownership	Percentage of Ownership	Net Value of Your Ownership
1. _____	_____	_____	_____
2. _____	_____	_____	_____
3. _____	_____	_____	_____
4. _____	_____	_____	_____
5. _____	_____	_____	_____
6. _____	_____	_____	_____
7. _____	_____	_____	_____

Total Current Value of Assets: $_____

LIABILITY INVENTORY

Description of Liability	Amount You Owe (Your Share of Liability)
1. _____	_____
2. _____	_____
3. _____	_____
4. _____	_____
5. _____	_____
6. _____	_____
7. _____	_____

Total Current Liabilities:	$_____
Total Assets	$_____
Less Total Liabilities	– _____
Total Value of Estate	$_____

4. The total value of your assets and whether your estate will be subject to federal estate taxes

If you discover that your estate will be subject to taxes, minimizing them should be one of your estate planning goals.

Ask for Directions: Where to Find Professional Help

Although the process of estate planning usually involves several professionals, including lawyers, financial planners, insurance agents, and accountants, estate planning does not have to be so complicated.

Although we do not recommend that you do it yourself, there are many helpful legal books, software programs, and clinics that will take care of most common situations. They are adequate if you have few assets and a limited number of people to whom you want these assets distributed. However, if you hold substantial assets or your wishes for bequesting your assets are complicated, you should seriously consider assembling a team of financial experts to make sure that your will covers every contingency. And because estate and probate laws vary from state to state, it is important to have your will drawn up in accordance with local laws by an attorney familiar with them.

▶ Mapping Your Final Trip: Creating a Will

Everyone needs a will. Actually, you need one or more of a series of legal documents that will protect you and your heirs in the event of your death or disability. Let's consider some of the myths that many people use as excuses for not having a will and the realities associated with each myth.

▶ *"We don't have children."* Okay, but you still have assets to pass on to your spouse, your other heirs, or charitable causes.

▶ *"We don't have enough assets."* Or, *"All of our assets are in retirement accounts with designated beneficiaries."* Even so, you may have minor children for whom you need to provide guardianship. It is also likely that some assets, such as vehicles, collectibles, and employer-provided life insurance, do not have designated beneficiaries. There may also be personal mementos that you want to leave to a particular family member or friend.

▶ *"It's too expensive to have a will prepared."* Actually, simple wills can be prepared professionally for a few hundred dollars. Do-it-yourself options also are available using ready-made forms and software programs. One caution: If you do it on your own, be sure that any online form or information that you use adheres to the laws in your state.

Your family structure also plays an important role in the need for a will. Almost all single or married people need a will. But it's even more important for anyone who has remarried to consider preparing a will or revising an existing one, especially if either spouse has children from a prior relationship. That's because intestate laws dictate disposition of assets and guardianships for minor children. (*Intestate* is the term that is used when a person dies without a will.) Every state has a generic will for residents who die intestate. Since it's written to cover most people, you may not like the choices that would be carried out on your behalf.

Your Will Is Not the Only Map You'll Need: Other Significant Documents

Even if you have a will, you're still not prepared properly for death or a sudden catastrophic accident. For most people, the odds of becoming medically or mentally incapacitated are actually higher than the odds of dying. This is an important fact to think about even if you're young because accidents happen to young people every day, unfortunately. Therefore, you also need a series of ancillary documents that address incapacity and other issues short of death, including a financial power of attorney and medical care documents.

Power of Attorney. Financial power of attorney, or durable power of attorney for finance, provides for the appointment of someone to make financial decisions for you. This power may go into effect immediately on signing the document, or it may be delayed until an event occurs that triggers the power, or until you are unable to manage your own financial affairs. This delayed activation is known as a *springing power.* Having this document eliminates the need for your family to petition the court to appoint a financial guardian or conservator.

Like all financial and legal decisions affecting your life, it is important to consider carefully to whom you give this power. Once in force, the individual with the power of attorney will be able to represent you in your financial affairs at any time. You also should consult with an attorney for rules that may be specific to your state of residence or domicile.

What to Pack

Information Your Lawyer Needs to Prepare Your Will

1. A list of your real estate property, such as your homes, and your tangible personal property, such as your cars and furniture, including how much you paid for them and where they are located. Bring deeds, bills of sale, and any other relevant documentation to prove your ownership. Also, indicate whether you own the property solely or jointly.

2. A list of intangible property, such as bank accounts, stocks, bonds, and mutual funds. Bring your latest bank and brokerage statements.

3. A list of all insurance policies and all pension and other employee benefits. Bring your latest statements.

4. A list of all your debts, including debts to banks, insurance companies, your employer, the IRS, and private individuals. Bring any documents outlining your liabilities.

5. The names, addresses, and telephone numbers of any professional you want contacted in the event of your death, such as your insurance agent, broker or banker, or another lawyer. Also bring the names, addresses, and phone numbers of the executor and any guardians named for your children. Include, of course, the names, addresses, and telephone numbers of your spouse and children.

6. Copies of all trusts that you and your spouse are grantors for or beneficiaries of.

7. Divorce decrees, property settlement agreements, and prenuptial and postnuptial agreements that you and your spouse may be parties to.

8. Any wills you may already have.

9. Any trusts you may have set up already.

Medical Documents. You should have two key medical care documents. The first is a directive to physicians, sometimes known as a living will or a health care proxy, which tells medical personnel what, if any, means of artificial life support you want and in what circumstances you want it, in the event of your medical incapacity. A living will and health care proxy only involves your health and has nothing to do with your financial situation or assets. It is activated when you become mentally or physically incapacitated and have no realistic hope of returning to your normal life.

The second medical document is a durable power of attorney for health-care, which names someone to make medical decisions on your behalf if you can't. Both of these documents can be created by a lawyer as part of your estate planning. You can save yourself headaches and additional needless heartache by doing your basic estate planning now. For more information on wills and estate planning, see *On the Road: Planning an Estate*.

▶ Two for the Road: Marital Property Laws

In the United States, there are two types of marital property law: community property and separate property. The type of marital property law recognized by your state dictates what is yours to give away and the inheritance rights of your surviving spouse.

Community Property States. With a few exceptions, if you are married and live in a community property state, you and your spouse each own one-half of the assets and money that each of you acquires together or separately during your marriage, regardless of whose name is on the ownership papers. Therefore, if you want your spouse to inherit your share of the community property, you have to transfer it to him or her in your will or through some other type of estate planning. Exceptions to community property include assets you inherit and gifts you receive while you are married. In addition, property you owned and income you earned prior to your marriage continues to be your separate property after you marry.

Generally, if you move from a community property state to a separate property state, the property and income you acquired while you were living in the first state remain community property. There are exceptions to the rules, however. For example, if you receive a gift or an inheritance of any size while you are married, it is your separate property, not community property, and you can do whatever you want with it when you are planning your estate. However, if you deposit your inheritance in an account that you share with your spouse, or if you commingle your separate property with your community property in some other way, the separate property can become community property. To avoid commingling, talk with an estate planning attorney.

In some community property states, community property does not have the right of survivorship. In other words, in these states, when you die, your

Hazard!

Keep Your Estate Plan and Will Up to Date

Review the following list periodically and discuss any shortcomings you find with your professional financial, tax, and legal advisors.

1. Do you have a written estate plan?

   Do you understand it?

   Has it been reviewed since you got married?

   Does it include an analysis of all potential strategies?

   Did you fully implement the selected strategies?

2. Do you have a will?

   Has it been reviewed since you got married?

   Was it updated when you moved to a new state, got married or divorced, had a baby, lost a parent, or experienced any other significant family change?

   Does your will name a guardian for your children if both you and your spouse are gone?

   Does your will create a trust and name a trustee to control assets for minor children if both you and your spouse are gone?

   Have you made appropriate provisions for any special needs children?

   Are you comfortable with the executor(s) and trustee(s) you selected?

3. Have you considered a living trust to avoid probate?

   If you have a living trust, have you retitled your assets in the name of that trust?

4. Have you delegated appropriate powers of attorney so that your affairs can be managed by the people you choose in the event of your mental or physical incompetence?

5. Are you taking full advantage of the marital deduction?

   Have you considered establishing a credit shelter (A/B or marital) trust?

   Have you retitled assets in the name of this trust?

6. Have you set up irrevocable life insurance trusts to ensure your life insurance proceeds are not taxed as part of your estate?

7. If you are a sole proprietor, a partner, or an owner of a closely held corporation, have you taken any of the following steps?

   Do you have a buy-sell agreement for the business?

Have you considered key person life and disability coverage? (insurance specifically for the most important executives or partners, without whom the business would probably fail)

Is there a written business continuation plan?

The bottom line: If you have taken the time to create a net worth, you need to complete the process by careful and skillful transition planning. Make sure your money goes to the people and causes you care about, in a time and manner you choose!

---

surviving spouse does not automatically inherit your half of the community property you share. Instead, you must use estate planning to effect that legal transfer: that is, if you want to ensure that your spouse gets your share of the community property when you die, you must specifically name your spouse as the beneficiary of your share in your will. Otherwise your spouse could end up sharing ownership of your community property with someone else, such as your child or perhaps another relative. (Obviously, your spouse's one-half interest will be unaffected by your death and vice versa. It will not be transferred to your child or other beneficiary; only your half will.)

Particularly if the asset were an important one, such as your home or car, this kind of ownership arrangement could create problems for your spouse. For example, your spouse might want to sell the asset or borrow against it, but the co-owner might disagree and prevent your spouse from doing what he or she wants with the asset.

In community property states, to help protect your spouse from disinheritance, you also cannot give away your spouse's half of the community property unless your spouse agrees to it. If you die without having conveyed your half of the community property to your spouse in your will or through some other legal mechanism, a state law may entitle your spouse to receive your full share anyway, unless you have children. If you have children, then your spouse and your children could end up as co-owners of your community property. This arrangement could be problematic if your spouse and children do not get along. Therefore, be sure not to overlook state laws concerning community property when you do your estate planning.

Community property can be changed into separate property. For example, you could give your community property to your spouse as a gift. To be certain that it is recognized as separate property, make the gift in writing.

Separate Property States. If you are married and live in a separate property state, the money you earn is yours only. Similarly, when you purchase an asset with your own money, you own it 100 percent and your spouse has no legal interest in it. If you both contribute money to buy an asset, you both own it legally, assuming that both of your names are on the title, deed, or other ownership documents.

However, if only your name appears on the ownership papers, you are the legal owner, not both of you. For example, assume that you and your spouse pool your money for a down payment on a new car and both of you contribute to the monthly payments. Despite the fact that both of you pay for the car, if only your name appears on the title, you legally own the car, not you and your spouse.

If you live in a separate property state, the law says that when you die, your surviving spouse is entitled to a fixed amount of your estate. If you don't leave your spouse at least that amount, he or she can "take against the will." That means that your spouse can exercise the right to take the fixed amount rather than the amount in your will.

Choosing Which Exit to Take: Estate Planning Tools

Roadmap 5.2 compares the advantages and disadvantages of the various types of estate planning tools. Roadmap 5.3 summarizes six ways to reduce your estate taxes.

Learn the Language

Definitions of Key Estate Planning Terms

Administrator The person appointed by a probate court to administer the estate of someone who has died without a will. An administrator plays the same role as an executor.

Beneficiary The person, charitable organization, pet, or other recipient who will inherit your money and other assets as laid out in your will, trust, custodial account, or the like.

Bequest A gift that is passed on according to the directions stipulated in a will.

Bond A legal document issued by a bonding or insurance company. A bond guarantees that if someone in a position of trust such as your executor,

Roadmap 5.2

Comparing Key Estate Planning Tools

Will

Advantages
▶ Easy and relatively inexpensive to prepare
▶ Allows a personal guardian and a property guardian to be named for a minor child
▶ Can be modified at any time up until death

Disadvantages
▶ Property subject to probate
▶ A minor automatically receives the asset(s) at ages 18 or 21, depending on your state. (You can get around this drawback by using your will to set up a testamentary trust for the minor. In the will you can specify at what age you want the minor to receive that property.)
▶ Probate often time-consuming and expensive

Joint Tenancy

Advantages
▶ Inexpensive and simple to use
▶ Avoids probate

Disadvantages
▶ Lack of full control over an asset you own as a joint tenant
▶ Making a solely owned asset a joint asset may incur gift taxes

Life Insurance

Advantages
▶ Safe, secure way to build an estate
▶ Avoids probate
▶ No income tax liability associated with benefits
▶ Good way to provide liquidity for estate

Disadvantages
▶ No flexibility governing when and how death benefits are paid to the beneficiary(ies) of your policy (You can deal with this disadvantage by designating a trust as the beneficiary of these proceeds. In the trust document you can spell out when and under what conditions the trust's beneficiary can receive the money.)

Roadmap 5.2 (continued)

Employee Benefits

Advantages
- ▶ Death benefits not subject to probate

Disadvantages
- ▶ No flexibility in how probate benefits are paid to the beneficiary(ies) of your benefits
- ▶ May be subject to taxes

Informal Bank Trust Accounts

Advantages
- ▶ Usually revocable
- ▶ Inexpensive and easy to set up
- ▶ Account funds not subject to probate

Disadvantages
- ▶ No flexibility in how or when account funds are paid to beneficiaries

Testamentary Trust

Advantages
- ▶ Provides tax advantages
- ▶ Allows control of when trust beneficiaries receive trust assets
- ▶ Not established until death

Disadvantages
- ▶ Trust assets probated before reaching trust

Revocable Living Trust

Advantages
- ▶ Avoids probate
- ▶ Offers control of trust assets while you are alive
- ▶ Possible to be both trustee and beneficiary of the trust
- ▶ Offers control of when a trust beneficiary receives trust assets and income

Disadvantages
- ▶ Relatively expensive to set up
- ▶ No tax advantages unless a revocable living trust is combined with a second trust that is designed to save on estate taxes, an option that adds extra expense

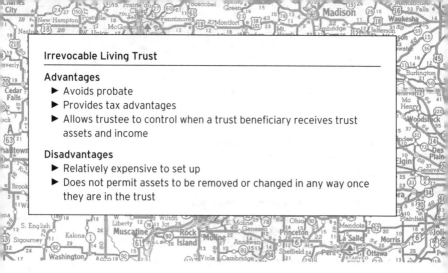

Irrevocable Living Trust

Advantages

▶ Avoids probate

▶ Provides tax advantages

▶ Allows trustee to control when a trust beneficiary receives trust assets and income

Disadvantages

▶ Relatively expensive to set up

▶ Does not permit assets to be removed or changed in any way once they are in the trust

account custodian, or trustee, fails to carry out his or her legal responsibilities, the company will pay a certain amount of money to whomever is harmed as a result.

Bypass Trust A type of trust used in conjunction with the unlimited marital deduction to reduce estate taxes.

Codicil An amendment to a will. Generally, codicils are used to make relatively small changes to a will. To be legally valid, a codicil must meet your state's legal requirements.

Community property Property acquired and income earned by a couple during their marriage, which is owned jointly by both spouses. In community property states, each spouse has a legal claim to one-half of all of the couple's property. Nine states are community property states: Arizona, California, Idaho, Louisiana, Nevada, New Mexico, Texas, Washington, and Wisconsin. The rest are separate property states.

Conservator A person appointed by the court to manage the financial affairs of an individual. Also called a *guardian*.

Custodian A person who is named to manage the assets placed in a custodial account set up for a minor child under the Uniform Gifts to Minors Act or the Uniform Transfers to Minors Act (see below).

Death taxes The taxes that your estate may have to pay after you die depending on its value. They are also referred to as *estate taxes*.

Disinheritance The exclusion of a family member from a will.

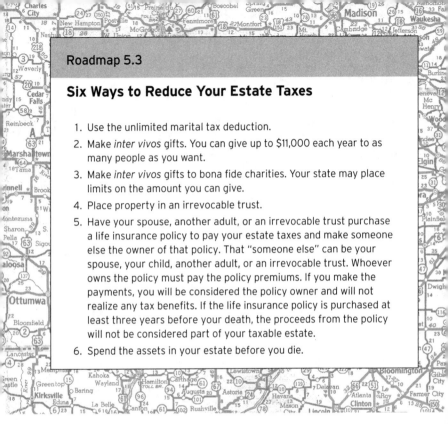

Roadmap 5.3

Six Ways to Reduce Your Estate Taxes

1. Use the unlimited marital tax deduction.
2. Make *inter vivos* gifts. You can give up to $11,000 each year to as many people as you want.
3. Make *inter vivos* gifts to bona fide charities. Your state may place limits on the amount you can give.
4. Place property in an irrevocable trust.
5. Have your spouse, another adult, or an irrevocable trust purchase a life insurance policy to pay your estate taxes and make someone else the owner of that policy. That "someone else" can be your spouse, your child, another adult, or an irrevocable trust. Whoever owns the policy must pay the policy premiums. If you make the payments, you will be considered the policy owner and will not realize any tax benefits. If the life insurance policy is purchased at least three years before your death, the proceeds from the policy will not be considered part of your taxable estate.
6. Spend the assets in your estate before you die.

Equity The difference between an asset's current market value and the amount of money that is owed on it.

Estate Everything that a person owns at the time of death.

Estate planning A multifaceted process that involves planning for the disposal of assets after death. Estate planning may also include taking steps to minimize the amount of estate taxes that your estate must pay in order to speed up the transfer of your assets to your beneficiaries. Estate planning may also include writing a living will and giving an appointed person a durable power of attorney for health care.

Executor The person you name in your will who will help settle your estate by taking it through the probate process after your death. Your executor also makes sure that the wishes you express in your will are carried out. Your choice for executor must be officially appointed by the court.

Gift tax A federal tax applied to inter vivos gifts. You get an annual gift tax exclusion of $10,000 ($20,000 if you and your spouse make a gift as a couple). The exclusion applies to as many individuals and organizations as you want to give to in any year. Gifts that are protected by the annual gift tax exclusion are not taxable and do not use up any of your unified gift and estate tax credit.

Holographic will A handwritten will.

Inheritance tax A tax paid by the beneficiary of an estate in some states.

Inter vivos gift A gift that you make to a beneficiary while you are alive.

Inter vivos trust Another name for a living trust.

Intestate Dying without a legally valid will.

Irrevocable trust A trust that cannot be changed once it is set up.

Joint tenancy A form of property ownership that allows two or more people to own a real estate asset together. One owner cannot give away his or her share of the property without the other owner's consent; and if one of the owners dies, the other owner(s) automatically own(s) the deceased's share. Married people often own property in this way, as do unmarried partners.

Living trust A trust that you set up while you are alive. It can be irrevocable or revocable, although most living trusts are revocable.

Living will A kind of health care directive that spells out your wishes regarding the specific types of end-of-life care and treatment you do and do not want.

Marital exemption A federal tax exemption that allows one spouse's estate to pass to the other spouse without any estate tax implications.

Payable-on-death account A bank account trust that you can use to leave funds to the account beneficiary. Also known as a Totten trust.

Personal guardian The person you name in your will to raise your minor child should both you and the child's other parent die.

Power of attorney A legal document that gives an appointed person the right to act on your behalf. A power of attorney may give this person the right to make financial decisions or health and medical care decisions for you. A power of attorney can also give an individual a one-time, temporary right to make decisions for you, or it can be a durable power, which means it lasts until you take it away.

Probate The legal process that proves the validity of your will, officially appoints your executor, pays your estate taxes if any are due, pays any legitimate creditor claims against your estate, and distributes the property in your will to your beneficiaries according to the terms of your will.

Probate estate All assets that you own that will go through the probate process.

Property guardian The person you name in your will to manage the property that you leave to your minor child if you die before your child is a legal adult.

Real property Real estate, including homes, other buildings, and land.

Residuary beneficiary The beneficiary named in your will who is entitled to receive any assets in your probate estate that are not specifically left to another beneficiary in your will, after all legitimate claims against your estate have been paid.

Residuary estate The assets left in your estate after all the assets with specific beneficiaries have been distributed. Also called the *residue of the estate.* These assets go to whomever you designate as the residuary beneficiary.

Revocable trust A living trust that can be modified or canceled after it is set up.

Self-proving will A will that includes a sworn statement from witnesses that it has been notarized.

Settlor The formal term for someone who creates a trust. Other terms used to describe this person include *trustor, grantor,* and *donor.*

Taking against the will An option given to surviving spouses to inherit a state-determined amount of their deceased spouses' estate rather than the assets that the deceased left them in their will.

Taxable Estate The assets in your estate that are subject to federal and state estate taxes after your death.

Tenancy by the entirety A form of joint property ownership that is available in some states to spouses only.

Tenants in common A type of joint property ownership that gives each owner a share of an asset without an interest in the shares of the other owner(s) or the right of survivorship. Owners can sell or give away their shares without the consent of the other owners.

Testamentary trust A trust that is part of your will and that is not funded until your death.

Testator The person who writes a will.

Trust A legal entity that you can create to own and manage assets for the benefit of one or more beneficiaries. The trust property is managed by a trustee and the trust beneficiaries take control of the property at a time specified in the document that establishes the trust.

Trustee The person who is named in the trust document to manage the trust assets.

Uniform Gifts to Minors Act or Uniform Transfers to Minors Act Federal laws that permit you to establish a custodial account for a minor child and to place certain types of assets in the account. A custodian manages those assets until the minor reaches ages 18 or 21.

Will A legal document that spells out what you want to have happen to the assets you own after you die. If you are the parent of a minor child, you can use your will to designate both a *personal guardian* and a *property guardian* for the child.

Traveling with Children

Saving for Your Kids' College Education

In May 2004, Opinion Research Corporation conducted a survey of college-bound teens and parents of college-bound teens on behalf of Fidelity Investments. The survey found that under ideal circumstances 93 percent of parents would be willing to help pay for their children's college education, with half willing to pay for all or most of the costs.

The best time to begin saving for your children's college education is before they are born. Realistically, though, most couples have other things on their minds when they're just starting out, and you probably have other short-term financial goals that you'd like to meet before you think about funding your children's education. Yet if you can implement prudent budgeting techniques before your children are born, you should be able to accrue the necessary money to help you reach your financial goals. This chapter describes how to estimate and calculate what you should save for each child's college education. It also describes various investment vehicles that can help you achieve this goal. Let's get started!

▶ What's the Toll? How Much Do You Need to Save for College?

Rather than dwelling on the hundreds of thousands of dollars that college educations may cost, you could put your mind at ease a bit by calculating how much you may actually pay for your child's education. Although it's hard to know what school your toddler might aspire to more than a decade from now, ask yourself the following questions:

1. Is your child more likely to attend a public university in the state where you live or an out-of-state public institution?
2. Is there a chance your child will enroll at a top-ranked private college, such as an Ivy League institution or its equivalent?
3. Are you thinking that your child may go to graduate school?
4. Are you considering a junior or community college for your child?

The more prestigious the schools that your children set their sights on, the more they will cost to attend, and the more you or your children will have to save or borrow to pay the tuitions. Many colleges and universities charge far less tuition than Ivy League schools. Less expensive institutions often provide high-quality educations, though they may not have the elite reputations. Sending your child to one of these institutions may ease some of the financial pressure.

Although you cannot answer the hypothetical questions posed above with much certainty, you can force yourself to confront the reality of determining how much you should save. Most parents save far less than they ultimately need for college costs, so if you can motivate yourself to invest more, you will be that much further ahead of most people in your situation. After all, what's the worst that could happen if you save too much? In the unlikely event that you accumulate more than enough money for college tuition, room, board, and other expenses, such as books and transportation, you will have plenty of other uses for the assets, like your retirement, for instance! However, if you save too little, you and your child will be forced to assume debt that will take years to repay and cost thousands of dollars in interest.

Quantifying the Typical Mileage: Calculating Average Future College Costs

How much you need to finance your child's undergraduate education primarily depends on the choice of college and its cost, the anticipated increase in the cost until your child reaches college age, and the likelihood of receiving financial aid.

The average nationwide cost of college attendance (tuition and fees, not including room and board) for the 2003–04 school year was $19,710 for a four-year private college and $4,694 for a four-year public university for an in-state resident (*Trends in College Pricing,* 2003, © 2003 by College Board). Add about $7,000 if the student attends an out-of-state public university, for a total of $11,740.

Multiply the national average annual cost by four years, and it costs $18,776 (for a public university) to $78,840 (for a private college) to send one child to four years of college today, not including room and board and annual price increases. The good news is that many students receive some sort of financial aid. The bad news is that much of the financial aid is in the form of loans, very few of which pay the full cost. If cost is an issue, determine your child's expectations regarding college no later than junior high school.

In addition, remember that college costs increase every year. For example, in the 2003–04 school year, average public university tuition and fees increased 14.1 percent, and private college costs rose 6 percent. Historically, college costs have climbed at about twice the annual inflation rate.

If your child is born today, and if college costs increase 5 percent per year for the next 18 years, the projected cost of a year at a public university by the time your child is a freshman is about $30,000. Based on a 6 percent return on your investments, you would need to save about $320 per month for the next 18 years to fund four years at a public university. For a private college, the cost in 18 years will be about $67,000, more than doubling your needed monthly

Tollbooth 6.1

How Much You'll Need to Save for College, Depending on Your Child's Current Age

	Cost of a Public College	Cost of a Private College
If Your Child is a	*You need to save*	*You need to save*
Newborn	$320/month	$690/month
Six-year-old	$440/month	$950/month
Twelve-year-old	$800/month	$1,700/month

savings to almost $700. Of course, these estimates are based on today's average costs. Individual college costs could vary significantly, requiring you to save more or possibly less. Tollbooth 6.1 shows a quick comparison.

The sooner you begin saving, the better. As mentioned, very few families actually save the full amount needed to pay for college. Colleges generally expect that you will save about one-third of the required amount, borrow one-third, and fund another third from your cash flow while the child is in college.

Quantifying Your Specific Mileage: Calculating Your Kids' Tuition

For a rough idea of how much college will cost and how much you must save, you can ask a financial planner to calculate the amounts, use a software program, or try one of the many calculators available on college financing Web sites. Most of these calculators require you to enter the number of years until your child starts college, the assumed inflation rate, the estimated return on your investments, and other factors to arrive at probable college costs. As you change your assumptions, note how the cost of college and the amount you must save change. A similar exercise is also available in Quicken, Microsoft Money, and other software packages described in Chapter 1. You may also want to check out http://www.collegeboard.com to access the calculators there that will help with your financial estimates.

Planning for a Long Journey: Investing Strategies and Vehicles

The higher the return that you earn on your savings and investments, the less money you must set aside for your children's college tuition. Unfortunately, because there are no guarantees of high returns in the investment world without commensurate high risks, you should put together a balanced portfolio of high-, medium-, and low-risk investments to fund your children's college educations. In general, as with all investments, the longer the time until you need the money, the more risk you can take in search of high returns. As the tuition bills draw closer and closer, you should take fewer and fewer risks so that all the money you will need is sitting in your money market account on the day you write your first huge check to the institution of your child's choice.

Which Way to Go? Ways to Save for College

Savings options are plentiful and confusing. Some plans pay interest and preserve your initial contribution or allow you to control how the savings are invested. Others do not. Adding to the confusion, how you save can affect your child's financial aid options. The most important thing is to begin saving, even if it's $25 a month. As your income increases, boost the amount you save.

Here's a quick overview of some ways to save:

▶ Section 529 savings plans
▶ Series EE and I savings bonds
▶ taxable accounts in a parent's name
▶ Coverdell Education Savings Accounts (formerly known as Education IRAs)
▶ retirement plans (401(k), traditional IRA, and Roth IRA)

Now let's look at each of these roads to a college education in more detail.

Section 529 College Savings Plans

Qualified tuition plans, also known as 529 plans, are a popular education savings method that feature special tax benefits and allow significantly greater contributions than other options, such as the Coverdell Education Savings Account (Coverdell ESAs). (For more on these savings accounts, see the next section of this chapter.) Every state now has at least one 529 plan. With so many choices, it's important to know the basics about how these plans work and what to consider before you invest.

These state-sponsored education savings programs allow parents, relatives, and friends to invest in a fund for your children's college education. Anyone can contribute money to a 529 plan on behalf of a beneficiary (student), and unlike Coverdell ESAs, contributors are not subject to income limitations, nor are there restrictions on the beneficiary's age. The only requirement is that amounts accumulated in the plan must be used to pay for the qualified education expenses of an undergraduate or graduate program at an accredited institution. Expenses that qualify include tuition, fees, books, supplies, required equipment, and room and board.

Each state designates a particular investment company to offer the plan to that state's residents, and the contributions are tax-deductible on your state income tax return. You can also invest in plans from other states, although no state tax deductions are available. Some of the firms that various states have chosen include American Century, Fidelity, Merrill Lynch, Putnam, Salomon Smith Barney, Strong, TIAA-CREF, T. Rowe Price, and Vanguard.

The firm invests the money in the account for you. In most states, you have a choice of investment alternatives; in other states, the manager makes all the investment decisions for you. In some states, you choose between aggressive, moderate, or conservative tracks; in other states, the investment manager will invest aggressively from the time your child is born until age 10. The manager will then invest increasingly conservatively until the money is in a money market fund by the time it is needed for tuition bills.

Keep in mind that investments in 529 savings plans fluctuate with the stock market, so they need to be monitored regularly just like retirement savings and other investments. You can change your investment selections or move the plan assets to another state's plan once a year.

Contributions to the Section 529 plan are tax deductible for the donor in their state of residence and not others. In all cases, the money in the account grows tax deferred until it is withdrawn for college fees and expenses. All withdrawals are untaxed if used for qualified expenses. If your first child decides not to go to college, the assets can be transferred to a second child and still retain the tax benefits. If you withdraw the money for noneducational purposes, you will be hit with a 10 percent penalty and have to pay income taxes on the money you take out.

Unlike other college savings plans, you can contribute a lot of money to a Section 529 plan. Individuals can contribute up to $55,000 per year ($110,000 per couple) per child. If you give $55,000 in one year, you must file a form with the IRS saying that this amount is in fact a gift of $11,000 a year over the next five years for gift tax purposes. There is a lifetime contribution limit per child that varies by state; for example, in Kansas, it is $127,000. If you contribute to a Section 529 plan, you cannot also contribute to a Coverdell Savings Account. This restriction is not a hardship because you can only give $2,000 to a Coverdell Savings Account anyway.

Requirements and Benefits of Section 529 Plans and Prepaid Tuition Plans

All 529 plans are subject to the requirements of the sponsoring state. Many states allow nonresidents to participate in their 529 plan. Among the benefits of a 529 plan are the following:

▶ *No federal income tax.* According to Section 529 of the Internal Revenue Code (which is how 529 plans got their name), earnings from plan investments are free from federal income tax as long as the funds are used to pay for qualified education expenses.

▶ *State tax deductions.* Some states allow a deduction for contributions to the state's 529 plan, others may tax out-of-state contributions, and still others follow the federal rules.

▶ *Estate planning advantages.* Most 529 plans are powerful estate planning tools. They allow individuals to make gifts of $11,000 annually to anyone without reporting the contribution or paying a federal gift transfer tax. According to a special provision of the plan rules, an individual can contribute up to $55,000 in one year to the plan without triggering the gift tax. This choice treats the gift as if it had been $11,000 per year spread over a five-year period. The only requirement is that no further gifts be made to that person for the next five years. A married couple can gift up to $110,000 per beneficiary in one year and reduce their taxable estate. A portion of the gift may be included in your taxable estate if you die within the five-year period.

These benefits, coupled with large contribution maximums (more than $200,000 in some states), make 529 plans attractive savings vehicles. However, if you use the money for anything other than qualified education expenses, you face a 10 percent penalty tax and taxes on the earnings subject to that distribution. Special exceptions apply if the student receives a scholarship, dies, or becomes disabled.

When choosing a 529 plan, take into account the following considerations:

1. *Eligibility.* Is the plan open to nonresidents?
2. *Fees and expenses.* Is there a sales commission, enrollment fee, or annual maintenance fee? Is there an asset-based management fee? What are the annual expenses of the underlying mutual funds?
3. *Investment considerations.* Does the plan use age-based or years-to-enrollment portfolios? Is there a fixed or guaranteed investment option? Can you build your own investment portfolio? How often can you change your investments? Who manages the plan's investments?
4. *Contributions.* What are the minimum initial and subsequent contributions allowed by the plan? What is the maximum contribution allowed? How much is deductible on my state income tax return?

5. *Time or age limitations.* Is there any limit on the age of the account beneficiary? How long can the account stay open? Are there restrictions on withdrawing funds from the plan?

A final consideration is the plan's impact on need-based financial aid. Prepaid plans are considered a student resource and result in a dollar-for-dollar reduction in financial aid. However, 529 Savings Plans are considered the owner's asset, not the beneficiary's. If the owner is the parent, up to 6 percent of the account's value will be included in the financial aid formulas. These plans are new, but it appears that private colleges may treat them as a student asset that will be assessed at 25 percent for financial aid formulas.

There are other considerations as well, so 529 plans may be most appropriate for families who do not expect to qualify for financial aid or who do not want to count on financial aid. An excellent Web site with information about all state-sponsored 529 Plans is http://www.savingforcollege.com.

Education Savings Accounts

Formerly the Education IRA, Coverdell ESAs provide tax incentives to save for a child's educational expenses. If you are within the income limits, you can contribute up to $2,000 per year for any child under the age of 18. Although the contributions are not deductible, the earnings grow tax free and are distributed tax free as long as they are used to pay for qualified educational expenses. If the funds are not used in this way, the earnings are subject to ordinary income taxes as well as a 10 percent penalty when withdrawn.

You can open a Coverdell ESA at most banks, mutual fund companies, or other financial institutions that offer traditional IRAs. There are some requirements, though:

1. Contributions must be made in cash or a cash equivalent, such as a personal check.
2. Contributions must be made by the due date of the contributor's tax return, with no extensions, usually by April 15.
3. The same beneficiary (the same child) can have multiple accounts, but total annual contributions cannot exceed $2,000. For example, if the parents contribute $1,500 to an account, the grandparents are limited to contributing $500. Excess contributions are subject to a 6 percent excise tax until they are withdrawn.
4. Life insurance contracts are not permitted.

5. Contributions can be made only if the beneficiary is less than 18 years old.
6. The money must be withdrawn or rolled over to a different family member within 30 days of either the beneficiary turning 30 years old (unless the beneficiary is a special-needs beneficiary) or the death of the beneficiary.
7. The definition of "family member," for the purpose of rollovers, includes the beneficiary's spouse, sibling, or other family member, up to and including first cousins of the beneficiary.

Contributions may be limited or phased out for higher-income individuals, based on a person's Modified Adjusted Gross Income (MAGI), which is the same as Adjusted Gross Income for most people. For example, in 2004, a single person with a MAGI of less than $95,000 can make the full $2,000 contribution; with a MAGI of $95,000 to $110,000, the contribution is pro-rated; and above $110,000 it's prohibited. For a married couple filing jointly, the phase-out range is $190,000 to $220,000. The income limits change periodically, so check with your tax advisor or IRS Publication 970, "Tax Benefits for Education," for the latest limits. If you're above the income limits, it's acceptable for another individual who is not, such as a grandparent, friend, or even the child, to make the contribution.

The definition of eligible schools has been expanded to include elementary and secondary schools (K–12), including public, private, or religious schools. Qualifying as institutions of higher education are colleges, universities, vocational schools, or post-secondary institutions, which are all eligible to participate in a student-aid program administered by the Department of Education. Qualified expenses include the following:

▶ tuition and fees, books, supplies, equipment, tutoring, and services for special-needs beneficiaries
▶ room and board, uniforms, transportation, and supplementary items and services, including extended day programs. (There are limitations on room expenses if a student lives off-campus or is not enrolled at least halftime.)
▶ computer equipment, Internet access, and educational software

Finally, keep in mind these important issues:

1. You can claim the HOPE or Lifetime learning credit in the same year that you take a tax-free withdrawal from a Coverdell ESA, but not for the same expenses.
2. Contributions to a Coverdell ESA and a 529 Plan may be made in the same year.
3. Coverdell ESAs are treated as a student asset, and withdrawals are counted as the student's income in determining financial aid eligibility. (Withdrawals are tax free.)
4. Once funds are contributed to a Coverdell ESA, they must be paid out to the beneficiary, and the gift cannot be revoked. The beneficiary can be changed, however.

The most significant advantages of Coverdell ESAs over 529 Plans are that they can be used for grades K–12, and they have more investment flexibility. If your child may be eligible for need-based financial aid in college, try to use up all of the money in the Coverdell ESA by December of the child's junior year in high school. For more information, check out the free IRS Publication 970, "Tax Benefits for Education," at http://www.irs.gov.

Tollbooth 6.2 is a comparison of some of the similarities and differences between the Coverdell and 529 plans.

Series EE and I Bonds

Series EE Savings Bonds purchased after December 31, 1989, and the new Series I Inflation Protection Bonds are two other ways to pay for college and save on taxes. If the required conditions are met, the interest from these bonds is tax exempt when used to pay for qualified educational expenses, which include tuition and fees but not room, board, and books.

Individuals can purchase up to $15,000 of Series EE bonds ($30,000 face value) and $30,000 Series I bonds (issued at face value) per year. Bonds must have been issued after December 31, 1989, to receive preferential tax treatment; the purchaser must be over age 24 at the time of purchase; and bonds must be purchased in the parents' names. If bonds previously purchased are titled incorrectly, there is a procedure to get them retitled, provided that the parents initially purchased the bonds and the parents' income is below the eligibility limits at the time of redemption. The bond's value is included in the bond owner's estate. Purchasing bonds in smaller denominations provides more flexibility because any redemption amount that exceeds the amount of qualified expenses loses its tax-free treatment.

Tollbooth 6.2

Comparison of Coverdell and 529 Savings Plans

Feature	Coverdell	529 Plan
Taxation of earnings if used for education	Not taxed	Not taxed*
Deductibility of contributions on federal and state taxes	No/No	No/Maybe (varies by state)
Annual contribution limit**	$2,000	None (subject to lifetime limits)
Subject to income limits	Yes (see above)	No
Beneficiary age restrictions	Yes (see above)	No
Can be used for grades K-12	Yes	No
Investment restrictions (generally)	Few	Many (varies by state)
Student asset or parent asset in financial aid formula***	Student	Parent
Revocable contributions	No	Yes

*If current rules are not extended, distributions after December 31, 2010, will be taxed at the beneficiary's tax rate; however, the law is expected to be extended.

**Gift tax rules apply; 529 plan has a special five-year gifting provision.

***Federal formula counts 529 assets as the parent's; some private colleges may count 529 assets as the student's; need-based financial aid may be affected.

Redemption must be in the year of qualified expenses. In your records, include the bond's serial number, face value, issue date, redemption date, total proceeds (principal and interest), receipt from the educational institution receiving the payment, and receipts for qualified expenses. Bond redemptions are reported on IRS forms 8815 and 8818.

Interest on the bonds can be partially or completely tax free, depending on the parents' income (indexed for inflation) in the year of redemption. For tax purposes, bonds are considered a parental asset, and the interest is deemed paid income. The IRS adds redemption interest to your income before determining eligibility for the tax break, which also affects your adjusted gross income (AGI) for financial aid purposes.

Savings bonds may appeal to families that expect to meet the income limitations at redemption, have a low risk tolerance and short time horizon, and are willing to accept the relatively low returns. More information is available at http://www.savingsbonds.gov or from the Bureau of Public Debt, PO Box 1328, Parkersburg, WV 26106-1328; Telephone: 1-877-811-7283; http://www.publicdebt.treas.gov.

Choosing the Right Vehicle: College Education Investment Options

In addition to the special savings plans for funding a child's college education, you can also invest in any of the traditional investment vehicles.

Growth Stocks or Growth Stock Mutual Funds. Over the long term, you'll earn the highest return from stocks with sharply rising earnings or from mutual funds that invest in growth companies. Individual growth stocks pay few or no dividends because they reinvest most of their profits in their companies to accelerate business growth. Individual stocks can perform spectacularly but can also plunge if competitors reduce the firm's profitability.

A safer and easier way to achieve rapid growth is to invest in growth-oriented mutual funds. These funds usually accept small amounts of money, such as $100 a month, which is a difficult amount to invest in individual stocks. Another important feature of growth funds is that fund managers attempt to buy the most promising growth stocks and sell the fading stars, so you have a good chance of achieving maximum returns. Though such funds are volatile from month to month or year to year, chances are that a well managed fund could provide an average annual return of 8 to 10 percent or more. Therefore, invest most of your college savings in growth stock funds for the first 10 to 12 years of your child's life.

Bonds or Bond Mutual Funds. Fixed income securities, or the mutual funds that invest in them, provide much more current income than stocks, but they have much less growth potential. If interest rates are very high (more than 6 percent), invest a significant percentage of your money in bonds to build a college fund. But if bonds yield only 3 to 5 percent, invest a smaller amount of your assets in them (perhaps up to 30 percent) while your child is young.

By the time your child becomes a teenager, you can put more money in bonds, which have less of a risk of falling sharply in value than stocks. Bond funds offer the advantage of a diversified portfolio and the ability to regularly buy small amounts. Because bond funds never mature, you never know exactly what a fund will be worth until you sell it. If you buy individual bonds, purchase those that mature in the year your child starts college, which will ensure a hefty amount of principal when you need it. To carry this strategy further, buy a series of bonds that will mature in each of the four years that your child attends college. Make sure that the bonds you buy are not callable (subject to recall by the borrower, through an early repayment of principal) before the date you need the money.

Zero-Coupon Bonds. Another way to make sure that a certain amount of principal will be available when you pay tuition bills is to purchase bonds known as "zeros," which are deeply discounted from their face value. The best strategy is to buy them so they mature when your child starts college. The higher the interest rate on the bond, the faster it will appreciate over time. Zeros come in two principal varieties: Treasuries and municipals.

Treasury zeros, usually called *STRIPS,* which stands for *separate trading of registered interest and principal of securities,* have no risk of default, cannot be redeemed before maturity, and usually pay higher yields than municipal bonds because they are federally taxable. The problem with STRIPS is that the IRS expects you to pay taxes every year on the growth of the bonds attributable to interest, even though you do not receive that interest in cash. This arrangement is more of a nuisance than a reason to avoid STRIPS, however.

If you buy a zero-coupon bond issued by a municipality, you can sidestep the tax problem altogether. Because the bond's interest is tax-exempt, you never owe taxes on the growth of the bond. However, be careful to select a zero-coupon municipal that cannot be redeemed before maturity. You do not want your well-laid plans upset by an early return of your principal.

Baccalaureate Bonds. A special purpose municipal zero-coupon bond, nicknamed a baccalaureate bond, is issued by more than 20 states to help residents pay for tuition at an in-state school. These bonds typically cost between $1,000 and $5,000 apiece, and mature between five and 20 years. It is best to buy one that matures in the year your child is expected to go to college. Unlike other municipal zeros, however, baccalaureate bonds cannot be redeemed early if interest rates fall.

Hazard!

Dangerous Road Ahead: Investments to Avoid

Several forms of savings and investments are frequently touted as being ideal for college savings but are truly inappropriate. A few examples include cash value life insurance, annuities, limited partnerships, unit investment trusts, and highly speculative devices such as options or futures. All of these options are designed to achieve other financial goals, such as insuring a life or providing retirement income, and are therefore inefficient and costly ways to pay for your children's college education.

Whether you assemble the money to pay for your children's college education from savings and investments, grants, scholarships, or loans, the costs are burdensome. The earlier you develop a plan to fund college, the more easily you will handle this burden. Although the sacrifice of paying for college is great, the reward of a bright future for your children can be even greater.

Baccalaureate bonds are extremely popular and usually sell out quickly when offered to the public. If you buy them when interest rates are high (more than 6 percent), they can be a good deal. However, compare the yields on baccalaureate bonds to those on EE savings bonds. The interest on baccalaureate bonds is exempt from federal and state taxes no matter what your income; with savings bonds, you receive a tax break only if your income falls beneath a certain limit. Therefore, if your income exceeds the limit, you will probably do better with baccalaureates. If your child decides not to attend an in-state school or go to college at all, you can cash in the bonds and use the proceeds however you choose.

Savings Bonds. As mentioned previously, although Series EE savings bonds do not have the growth potential of growth mutual funds, they can provide a solid base for funding at least a part of your child's college education. Savings bonds formerly had a guaranteed minimum rate, but that policy was discontinued in May 1995. The yields on savings bonds issued on May 1, 1997, or later are based on 90 percent of the average yields of five-year Treasury securities for the preceding six months. Series EE bonds increase in value every month and interest is compounded semiannually. Therefore, if interest rates rise, savings bond returns will also rise, but if rates fall, yields will drop. Savings bonds are easy to accumulate and sometimes available through a payroll savings plan in denominations as small as $25.

Series EE bonds also offer a special advantage to parents saving for their children's education. If your modified adjusted gross income at the time you redeem your savings bonds is between $55,750 and $70,750 for individuals or between $83,650 and $113,650 for married couples filing jointly (amounts are adjusted slightly for inflation every year), the interest you earn from the bonds is either fully or partially tax exempt if you use that interest for college tuition for either yourself, your spouse, or your children. The bonds must be redeemed in the same calendar year that tuition and fees are paid. Make sure to secure the bonds in the parents' names, not the child's name, if you want to take advantage of this tax break. This type of savings bond is called an education bond, and it can apply to any bond purchased after December 31, 1989. For more information on how savings bonds can be used to finance college education, take a look at the U.S. Treasury's savings bond Web site at http://www.savingsbonds.gov.

Paying Tolls

Handling Taxes as a Married Couple

When you get married, not only do your day-to-day finances change, but your tax situation is transformed as well. Other chapters have touched on some of the different tax situations facing you. For example, Chapter 4's analysis of retirement planning strategies suggested ways that you can arrange for taxes to be deferred on your investments. This chapter, however, covers some general tax issues that married couples should be aware of, most of which are benefits! So let's hit the road.

▶ Different Tolls: Tax Rates and Tax Brackets for Married Couples

Taxes are probably the most unpleasant aspect of personal finance. However, just because you do not like thinking about how much you must pay in federal, state, and local taxes every year does not mean that you should avoid the subject. If you pay little or no attention to the tax consequences of every financial move you make, you will certainly owe the government more money, not less.

On the other hand, if you learn basic tax-saving strategies, you can maximize the amount of money you spend and invest while you minimize your tax bite. The two basic tax-saving approaches include delaying the payment of taxes, using tax-deferral strategies, and sidestepping taxes altogether. If you concentrate on learning the thousands of pages of complex tax laws and regulations, you will surely be overwhelmed. The fact is, most obscure tax laws do not apply to the typical taxpayer. However, you should understand basic tax strategies; know how to file your taxes; and implement the best methods to cut your tax bill, including legal deductions, credits, and other tax-sheltered plans. Even if a tax preparation professional fills out your return, you are the one who must act in a tax-smart manner throughout the year.

You need to file a tax return, of course, unless you meet certain age and income restrictions. For married couples filing jointly, you must file if

- ▶ you are both younger than age 65 and earn at least $12,950,
- ▶ one spouse is age 65 or older but you earn at least $13,800,
- ▶ both spouses are age 65 or older but you earn at least $14,650.

Most married couples file jointly. If you are married and filing your tax returns separately, you must file regardless of age if you earn at least $2,800. (A couple might file separately if they like to keep their financial affairs distinct.)

Tollbooth 7.1 shows the tax rates and tax brackets for 2005 (the latest year available). Note the difference between the two tax categories "married filing jointly" and "married filing separately."

> *If you and your spouse each have income, you may want to figure your tax both on a joint return and on separate returns (using the filing status of married filing separately). You can choose the method that gives the two of you the lower combined tax.*

The tax code offers married couples many advantages. For example, married couples filing jointly move into higher tax brackets at higher levels of income than single people.

You can choose married filing separately as your filing status if you are married. This filing status may benefit you if you want to be responsible only for your own tax or if it results in less tax than filing a joint return. However, you will generally pay more combined tax on separate returns than you would on a joint return. The IRS says that you must file separately if

Tollbooth 7.1

2005 Tax Rates

If taxable income is over	But not over	The tax is
Married, filing jointly		
$0	$14,600	10% of the amount over $0
$14,600	$59,400	$1,460.00 plus 15% of the amount over 14,600
$59,400	$119,950	$8,180 plus 25% of the amount over 59,400
$119,950	$182,800	$23,317.50 plus 28% of the amount over 119,950
$182,800	$326,450	$40,915.50 plus 33% of the amount over 182,800
$326,450	no limit	$88,320.00 plus 35% of the amount over 326,450
Married, filing separately		
$0	$7,300	10% of the amount over $0
$7,300	$29,700	$730 plus 15% of the amount over 7,300
$29,700	$59,975	$4,090 plus 25% of the amount over 29,700
$59,975	$91,400	$11,658.75 plus 28% of the amount over 59,975
$91,400	$163,225	$20,457.75 plus 33% of the amount over 91,400
$163,225	no limit	$44,160.00 plus 35% of the amount over 163,225

Source: http://www.irs.gov/formspubs/article/0,,id=133517,00.html

▶ you and your spouse have different fiscal years in which you must report taxes,
▶ one spouse is a nonresident alien,
▶ either spouse is claimed as a dependent on someone else's return.

If and when you have children, you can claim an exemption for each child, which will lower your tax bill. However, these exemptions are phased out if your income is high enough.

The tax law establishes other rules for couples as well. For example, if one spouse does not have earned income, he or she can still contribute up to $4,000 in a spousal individual retirement account (IRA), on top of $4,000 to a regular IRA.

You can claim at least one exemption for everyone in your household. If you are married with dependent children, you can claim an exemption for yourself, your spouse, and each of your children. You can also claim an exemption for a dependent parent living with you. (The parent is a dependent if you provided at least 50 percent of his or her income in the past year.)

Drive Carefully: Tax Deductions You Can Legally Take

To lower your taxable income, you will want to take steps to qualify for as many deductions as possible. Remember, however, when you take a deduction, it lowers your taxes by your marginal tax rate. Therefore, the lower your tax rate, the less money you save from each additional deduction.

Here's a simplified example. If you have $1,000 worth of mortgage interest deductions, and you pay taxes at a 50 percent marginal rate, the value of the deductions is $500. If your tax rate drops to 30 percent, the value of that same $1,000 is $300. So when you pursue deductions, keep in mind how much they will actually save you in taxes.

Each year everyone qualifies for the standard deduction, which is the part of your income on which you do not pay taxes. Here are the standard deductions for 2005. Each year, these amounts are adjusted slightly for inflation:

▶ $9,700 married filing jointly
▶ $4,850 married filing separately

If your and your spouse's individual deductions total more than the standard deduction, it makes sense to itemize individual deductions. However, if your income is above a certain level ($142,700 if filing jointly; $71,360 if filing separately), you may not get the full benefit of your deductions.

The following deductions are not subject to the overall limit on itemized deductions:

▶ Medical and dental expenses
▶ Investment interest expense

- ▶ Casualty and theft losses from personal use property
- ▶ Casualty and theft losses from income-producing property
- ▶ Gambling losses

If your itemized deductions are subject to the limit, the total of all your itemized deductions is reduced by the smaller of:

- ▶ 3 percent of the amount by which your AGI exceeds $142,700 ($71,350 if married filing separately), or
- ▶ 80 percent of your itemized deductions that are affected by the limit.

The following deductions are subject to the limit. You may wish to consult with your accountant or financial advisor if you are affected by the limits.

Casualty and Theft Losses. If you have suffered a major property loss due to damage or theft and are not reimbursed by an insurance policy, you may qualify for a deduction.

Charitable Contributions. You can deduct contributions made to qualified charities in cash, securities, real estate, or physical property. At a certain level (check with your accountant or the IRS for the current level), you must get a written receipt from the organization to substantiate your claim. A canceled check is not enough proof for the IRS. (More on charity later in this chapter.) You can accumulate deductions by donating cash or property to qualified charities. If you donate an asset, such as stocks, bonds, or real estate that has appreciated sharply, you avoid the capital gains taxes you would have paid had you sold the asset for a profit, and you then qualify for a charitable contribution deduction. Finally, if you do volunteer work for a charity, you can also deduct your unreimbursed expenses, such as the travel costs involved in doing your job.

Interest Expenses. You may be paying five kinds of interest that can generate deductions: home mortgage interest, points on a mortgage, interest on business loans, investment interest, and interest on student loans. Consumer interest, such as the interest you pay on credit cards or on car or personal loans, is no longer deductible. (The next section of this chapter tells more about tax breaks from owning your home.)

Medical Expenses. You can deduct unreimbursed medical expenses that exceed 7.5 percent of your AGI. The IRS has issued a long list of the medical expenses that are deductible.

State, Local, and Foreign Taxes. You can deduct any income taxes you have paid to your state, your locality, or a foreign government. In addition, all state, local, and foreign real estate taxes are deductible on your federal return.

Miscellaneous Expense Deductions. The IRS has approved as deductible many other expenses, all falling in the miscellaneous category. To qualify for this deduction category, all miscellaneous expenses must total at least 2 percent of your AGI. In general, the expenses that qualify as miscellaneous deductions are those related to the performance of your job for which your employer will not reimburse you, such as equipment costs, dues and subscriptions, uniforms and work clothing, and many others.

Expenses Incurred When Starting a Business. As long as you can show the IRS that you are trying to profit from a business venture that you start, many expenses legitimately incurred by your company qualify for business-related deductions. For example, you can deduct the business-related portion of your car lease payments. You can also deduct certain travel and entertainment expenses, and the cost of a home office if it is your only place for meeting customers and conducting the business. However, if you don't profit in three out of five consecutive years, the IRS may claim that you are pursuing a hobby and not running a legitimate business. You may be able to counter this claim by documenting all the steps you have taken to become profitable.

Traveling Home: Tax Breaks from Home Ownership

Most people only think of taxes in a negative way. However, when you own your own home, you actually get some positive benefits. In fact, the home is probably the best tax shelter available to most Americans! So let's look at some of the tax-related possibilities of first-time home ownership.

Before we hit the road, two caveats. First, tax calculations are complicated, and it's important that you don't take this information as a guide to doing your own taxes. For your own tax preparation, you need a competent accountant or a tax lawyer. This section is only an overview that shows some of the possibilities; check with a professional for your specifics.

Second, it's important to understand that the following information pertains to your principal residence and sometimes a second home. In fact, you can only deduct the mortgage interest on a maximum of two homes as a married couple. A person can have only one principal residence, and it usually is defined as the place where you spend most of your time. A second home is generally a vacation home that you visit occasionally. This distinction may seem overly simplified, but some people have homes or condos that they rent out, and the rules for rental property are quite different and beyond the scope of this book. So again, this tax information pertains to your main home, your principal residence.

On to our destination: Home ownership offers a number of tax breaks. On your Schedule A (the IRS form that lists your itemized deductions), you can deduct

▶ mortgage interest (on your principal residence and a second home),
▶ property taxes,
▶ points paid on a new loan,
▶ points paid on a refinanced loan (must be amortized over the life of the loan).

In addition, if you sell your home at a profit, capital gains of up to $500,000 for married couples filing jointly are tax free ($250,000 per person), as long as you have lived in your principal residence at least two of the last five years (more on capital gains in the next section). Better yet, you can use this same exemption again after living in another home for at least two years of the previous five.

Many people buy a home primarily for the financial and tax incentives, which can include not only the mortgage interest tax and property tax deductions just mentioned but also capital gains exclusions and penalty-free IRA withdrawals for first-time homebuyers. Owning a home may also enable you to itemize your deductions, which opens up an array of other deductible expenses. Let's look at each of these incentives in a bit more detail.

Reducing the Toll: Deducting Your Mortgage Interest and Property Taxes

As mentioned, one of the enduring benefits of home ownership is the federal tax deduction for interest and real estate taxes. For example, on a home with a $100,000 mortgage, the deductions will total about $8,000 per year, and, depending on your tax bracket, they will reduce your federal taxes by $1,200 to $3,200. This amount will decrease as you pay down the loan. If you have an ARM (adjustable-rate mortgage), the amount may go up in the event your interest rate increases. Consult with an accountant, tax attorney, or an

IRS advisor for the proper way to file your taxes, especially for the year that you get a new mortgage.

The basic tax benefit for home ownership is simple to calculate: For each dollar that you spend toward your mortgage interest and property taxes, you are entitled to subtract a dollar from your adjusted gross income (on which you pay taxes). Use the following formula to calculate your potential savings:

> Monthly Mortgage Interest Payment
> + Monthly Property Tax Payment
> = Subtotal
> × Your Effective Tax Rate
> = Monthly Tax Savings

> Monthly House Payment
> − Monthly Tax Savings (calculated above)
> = Real Cost of Monthly House Payment

In the first year of home ownership, you may also be entitled to an additional tax break if you paid any points (also called origination fees) to the lender to get your mortgage loan. The points are considered prepaid mortgage interest and can be deducted as additional mortgage interest. You can amortize them over the term of your mortgage or take them in the first year of home ownership. The maximum amount of interest that you can deduct on a home mortgage, as of this writing, is $1 million total, even if you have two homes.

If, after you purchase your new home, you decide to get a home equity mortgage, and you use the money for anything other than home improvement or building, you are further limited in how much interest you can deduct. You are limited to a maximum mortgage for other purposes of $100,000.

One question that sometimes arises involves how much mortgage interest you can pay in one year. For example, you normally have 12 monthly payments and you deduct the interest paid on all of them. But what if you made the following January's mortgage payment in late December, and it was cashed by the lender before December 31? Because interest is paid in arrears (after it's due), you would be entitled to deduct 13 months' interest instead of 12. This difference could give you a hefty extra deduction in that year and, indeed, many owners take advantage of this benefit. (The full amount of interest you have paid should show up on a statement from the lender that will probably be mailed to you in January.) The drawback is that during the next year you would have only 11 monthly payments of interest to deduct (unless you again made the January payment early).

You can also take a deduction for the property taxes you pay. The taxes on both your principal residence and a vacation home are fully deductible from your personal income taxes. Furthermore, the property taxes are deductible in the year that you pay them. In most cases property taxes are payable in December and March. If, in December, you make the payment for the following March, you can take the deduction for both payments on that year's taxes, again receiving a one-time tax deduction boost. This method only applies, of course, if you make your own tax payments. If your tax is paid out of an impound (an escrow account), then it's normally paid in two installments, and you can't take advantage of early payment.

Other Considerations for Tax Deductions on Your Home

When you buy a home, your paycheck actually increases. Because you now have mortgage interest and property tax deductions, you'll owe less federal income tax. You can take home that savings each month by increasing the number of personal deductions you take with your employer! Making the calculations, however, can be tricky. You want to get as much as you're entitled to, but if you take too much, you could end up owing more money and possibly incur penalties on April 15.

There are some things homeowners can't deduct. You can't deduct your fire or homeowners insurance nor the maintenance of your home. Your bills for gardeners and water won't get you a write-off. You also can't deduct the cost of fixing a water heater or repairing the roof, no matter how much they cost, although you can deduct improvements that you have added to your home, such as a new kitchen, new deck, or new chimney (discussed later in this chapter).

A Toll-Free Highway: Penalty-Free IRA Withdrawals for First-Time Homebuyers

If you have an IRA, you may be entitled to withdraw funds from the IRA penalty free for the down payment on a home. But the early withdrawal is subject to income taxes on any previously untaxed distributions. A distribution from a Roth IRA is not subject to the early distribution penalty or income tax, but it must first meet a five-year holding requirement. Before withdrawing any funds, be sure you have met the requirements to qualify for this distribution treatment, and that you have weighed the potential effect on your retirement savings. (Refer to Chapter 4 on retirement planning.)

Farther Down the Road: Capital Gain Exclusion When You Sell Your Home

Hopefully, you will make money on your home. It's important to remember, however, that homes do not always appreciate in price. For example, during the early 1990s, the value of most homes in the country declined. Although you generally pay taxes on a gain, you cannot take a write-off on your taxes for a loss on the sale of your home.

If the price of your home goes up, you probably will be able to take advantage of one of the biggest tax benefits available in the country: the personal residence exclusion. When you sell your home, this tax break allows you to exclude the proceeds of the sale from your taxable income up to $500,000 if you're married and file jointly, and up to $250,000 if you're single, or married and filing separately.

There are a few requirements for taking advantage of this exclusion. The home must have been your principal residence for two of the previous five years. If you lived there less than two years, you may still be able to claim some portion of the exclusion if you were forced to sell because of a change in the location of your employment, a health condition, or some other unforeseen circumstance. In that event you would get only part of the $500,000 exclusion for married couples filing jointly. Finally, you can claim the exclusion only once every two years.

Let's take an example to be sure we're clear about how this exclusion works. Let's say you and your spouse buy your first home and live in it for at least two years. It just so happens that you bought in a great location for price appreciation, and you've seen the value of your home skyrocket. At the end of the two-year period, it's gone up nearly $100,000. Your tax advisor or accountant tells you that you've got a capital gain of $97,000. How much tax do you owe on that gain? The answer is nothing whether you're single or married! If the gain had been $197,000, you would still owe no taxes, again whether you're single or married. Similarly, if the gain had been $497,000 and you were married filing jointly, no tax would be due.

If, however, your gain was over $500,000, then you'd owe capital gains tax on the overage, or the amount that's over the $500,000. For example, if the gain was $550,000, you'd owe capital gains tax on the $50,000 excess. What can you do with the gain? Anything you like. You do not have to reinvest it in another house.

How to Determine Your Gain When You Sell. Determining your gain is not as easy as it may seem. The gain is not what you might consider the profit on the sale. Instead, it is calculated using a specific government formula. Here's how it works:

All property, as far as the IRS is concerned, has a "basis." This is usually what you paid for the property. In terms of your first home, your basis is usually the price that you bought it for plus your costs of purchase, which include closing costs and loan costs that are not deductible immediately. Your basis is also increased by any improvements you made to the property.

For example, let's say you buy a home for $125,000 and your costs of purchase amount to another $5,000. Your basis is now $130,000. But let's say that you add a room, improve the kitchen, and build a fence for a total cost to you of $15,000. Now your basis has jumped up to $145,000:

Price	$125,000
Costs	+ 5,000
Basis	$130,000
Improvements	+ 15,000
Adjusted basis	$145,000

The importance of increasing your basis becomes apparent when you calculate your gain. Let's say that you sell your property for $240,000. You have sold for more than you paid, so you will have a taxable gain or profit. How much is it?

Let's say that it cost you $15,000 for the commission and closing costs to sell your property. When computing your gain, you are allowed to adjust the sales price to account for some costs of the sale.

Sales price	$240,000
Sales costs	− 15,000
Adjusted sales price	$225,000

Now you can calculate your gain on the sale of your home: Subtract your adjusted basis from your adjusted sales price.

Adjusted sales price	$225,000
Adjusted basis	– 145,000
Taxable gain	$ 80,000

Finally, how much tax do you pay on the gain? Zero, if you qualify for the personal residence exclusion. If not, you would pay tax on the $80,000 gain, which is why it's important to keep track of improvements you make to your property. Remember, improvements increase your basis and thus reduce your taxable gain. Also keep in mind that you may live in your house much longer than the two-year minimum, and after 10 or 20 years of inflation, your profit could indeed exceed the maximum exclusion. Again, any improvements added to your basis will reduce your taxable gain and may keep you within the exclusion limits.

What Constitutes an Improvement to Your Home? Anything that adds value to your property is probably an improvement. It's important to remember, however, that repairs and maintenance are not improvements. If you repair a roof, it's not an improvement. If you've reseeded your front lawn, it's not an improvement. However, if you put on a new, different, and more expensive type of roof, it might be considered an improvement. And if you put in expensive landscaping, it might also be considered an improvement. You should check with an accountant to be sure if your improvements qualify.

More Toll-Free Roads: Other Home Tax Savings

As you can see, when you become a homeowner, you enter the world of tax planning and legitimate tax avoidance in a big way. As a renter, the most tax planning you may do is occasionally adjusting the personal deductions on your W-4 form. Perhaps you go to the corner tax preparer to get your tax return prepared. Unless you are self-employed, that is all you have to do.

With a house, there are lots of tax considerations. You may even decide that the tax advantages of owning property are so good that you would like to buy a second house to rent out. A great many first-time buyers quickly move on to become first-time landlords. If that's the case for you, see "Recommended Resources" in Appendix B.

Deducting Your Moving Costs. Many people don't realize that a portion of their moving costs may be deductible from their federal income taxes. It depends why you're moving and how far. If the move is job related, and if your new home is more than a certain number of miles from your old home (a distance determined by the IRS), you may be able to deduct all of your moving costs up to a maximum amount. You may also be able to deduct some mortgage costs that are not normally deductible.

The rules on housing deductions change frequently, so check with http://www.irs.gov to see if you are eligible for any of these or other deductions.

▶ Alternate Routes to Avoid Tolls: Tax Credits

The best tax-saving device is a tax credit, which lowers your tax bill by one dollar for every dollar of credit you receive. Therefore, if you receive a $1,000 credit, you can take $1,000 off your tax bill. A tax credit is far better than a deduction, which lowers your taxes only by your marginal tax rate. Here are just a few tax credits of interest to married couples.

Route #1: The Earned Income Tax Credit

The earned income tax credit either reduces your taxes or results in a refund if you earn too little to owe taxes. You don't have to have children to claim the credit. The more you earn, the less credit you receive. To find out the amount of the credit you may qualify for, look at the IRS "Earned Income Credit (EIC) Table," which is updated annually. The following paragraphs describe some other tax credits that married couples should be aware of.

Route #2: Child Tax Credit

There are various tax benefits associated with having children. You can qualify for a Child Tax Credit, the Hope Scholarship, and Lifetime Learning Credit for your children. Under certain circumstances, interest on student loans may be deductible as well. You also may be able to save up to $500 a year tax free in an Education IRA for your children. (See Chapter 6 for more information on tax savings on your children's education costs.)

The credit for which you are most likely to qualify pertains to dependent and child care expenses. Because you're just getting married, you might not be ready to think about having children, but you still might want to know something now about the tax breaks of doing so. The Child Tax Credit is designed to help ease the financial burden of caring for your dependents. If you pay for more than half of the yearly expenses of a child (or another dependent, such as a parent), you can qualify for a credit based on a percentage of your expenses.

Your child must be a U.S. citizen and can be your own child, a grandchild, a stepchild, or a foster child whom you can claim as a dependent. However, the credit is phased out if your modified adjusted gross income is more than a certain level; check with the IRS for the most up-to-date information.

You can claim a deduction for your new baby on your income tax form in the form of a child tax credit. To smooth the tax issues, apply for a Social Security number for your child as soon after birth as possible. You'll need to file a Form SS-5 with the Social Security Administration. Most hospitals assist you with this form after the birth of your baby.

Regardless of your filing status, you can claim a per child tax credit if your dependent child (under age 17) is a U.S. citizen or resident. However, the credit may be phased out for higher-income families.

In addition, depending on your income level, you may be entitled to a credit on some of your expenses for qualified child care while both you and your spouse work or look for work. Taxpayers with higher income levels might opt to use an employer's Flexible Spending Account (FSA) for dependent care expenses, if available (more about FSAs later in this chapter). In an FSA, contributions are taken out of your salary before federal income taxes, Social Security taxes, and most state and local taxes. You end up paying fewer taxes and have more money available on payday.

Route #3: Adoption Credit

You can also earn a credit if you adopt a child under age 18, or someone who is mentally or physically handicapped. The adoption of a child with special needs can qualify you for an even greater tax credit. This credit is phased out if your adjusted gross income is above a certain level; again, check with the IRS for the most up-to-date information. To claim the adoption credit, you must show what your adoption expenses included, such as court costs, attorney fees, adoption fees, travel expenses, and other expenses directly related to the legal adoption of an eligible child.

If you adopt a U.S. child, you must claim the credit in the year after you incur the expense, or the year the adoption becomes final, whichever comes first. However, if you adopt a foreign child, the deduction can only be taken if and when the adoption is completed. Some employers also offer adoption assistance programs that can be used in conjunction with the adoption credit. For more information, check out the following Web sites:

► http://www.babycenter.com
► http://www.4woman.gov
► http://www.childrentoday.com
► http://www.parenthood.com/links.html

Putting on the Brakes: Individual Retirement Accounts

You can save a significant amount of taxes in the long run by maximizing your use of all of the different types of IRA accounts available to you. Depending on the IRA and your income level, you may be able to deduct your initial contribution, but most important in the long run is your ability to have the earnings grow tax deferred in a regular IRA and tax free in a Roth IRA, as long as you hold the assets in a Roth for at least five years.

For regular tax-deductible IRAs, you can earn a full or partial deduction if your income is up to $100,000 in 2007 for a married couple filing jointly if you are a participant in an employer-provided retirement plan. You will pay taxes on your IRA distributions when you withdraw the money in retirement after age 59½.

With the Roth IRA, you do not get a deduction up front, but you can withdraw the capital in retirement totally tax free. Unlike regular IRAs, you do not have to start taking money out of a Roth IRA at age 70½. You can, in fact, keep it in the account forever and pass on the proceeds to your beneficiaries tax free.

Note: You also can save on taxes by establishing an Education Savings Account for your children. You can contribute up to $2,000 per year for each child in your household up to the age of 18. That limit is reduced if you report an adjusted gross income of more than $150,000 for a married couple filing jointly. Assets inside an ESA grow tax free and can be withdrawn tax free as long as the proceeds are used to pay for education expenses at a post-secondary school.

If you are self-employed, you can contribute even more to an IRA-like vehicle, such as a Keogh, SIMPLE, or SEP plan that gives you an up-front deduction and tax-deferred growth.

Preparing for the End of Your Journey: Retirement and Estate Planning Tax Issues

The unlimited marital tax deduction gives married people a break on their federal estate taxes. It allows you to leave all of your estate to your spouse without incurring any estate tax liability, regardless of your estate's value.

Although this deduction provides an immediate benefit to your surviving spouse, without careful estate planning, it can create future tax problems for your spouse's estate. In fact, the use of the unlimited tax deduction only postpones the payment of your estate taxes, which will have to be paid by the estate of your surviving spouse when he or she dies.

Before taking this route, talk with an estate planning attorney. The attorney may recommend that you set up a trust to get around the problem. As discussed in Chapter 5, many estate planning goals can be achieved by using a trust. In addition, by establishing various kinds of trusts, you can sidestep estate tax bills. See Chapter 5 for more information about estate planning.

Sharing the Driving: Shifting Income to Your Children

You can also reduce the total amount of taxes your family pays by transferring a tax burden from someone in a high tax bracket to someone in a lower tax bracket. Again, to sidestep gift taxes, such gifts must not exceed $11,000 each.

Before the Tax Reform Act of 1986, there were many more income-shifting strategies than there are today. Nevertheless, you can still shift some income-producing assets to your children who are younger than age 14. The first $700 of unearned income (the income generated by stock dividends and bond interest, as opposed to money a child earns by working a paper route, for example) goes completely untaxed. The next $700 of unearned income is taxed at the child's rate, which is usually less than half of the parents' rate. However, any unearned income that the child receives that exceeds $1,400 is taxed at the parents' rate. This tax is usually known as the *kiddie tax.*

Once your child turns 14 years old, all of his or her unearned income is taxed at the child's rate, which may open up some income-shifting possibilities. For example, you might give your child a gift of $11,000 or less to invest for college. Your spouse could donate another $11,000. Realize, however, that you relinquish control of that money, and your child can do whatever he or she likes with it once the child reaches the age of majority, which is usually age 18.

On the Road to Work: Tax Breaks from Your Employee Benefits Plan

Many companies offer employee benefits in the form of what is known as a cafeteria plan, which allows you to customize your employee benefits package to better meet your individual needs. This arrangement is especially helpful for married couples because they can decide whose employer offers the best and most benefits. So be sure that you and your intended review both your benefit plans carefully, paying special attention to your health insurance premiums, co-pays, and deductibles, as well as the amount of your employer's retirement plan's matching contribution.

You can shelter some of your investment capital from taxes until you retire, when you probably will be in a lower tax bracket. You can contribute to Keogh plans, 401(k) or 403(b) salary reduction plans, simplified employee pension (SEP) plans, IRAs, and profit-sharing plans. Certain fringe benefits, such as the first $50,000 of group life insurance coverage and medical insurance premiums paid by your employer, are not taxed.

Flexible Spending Accounts. Many companies also offer flexible spending accounts (FSAs) that allow you to put aside pretax money from your paycheck to cover certain health care and dependent care costs. It's a win-win situation for you and your employer: You win because you save money by paying for only the benefits you need with untaxed dollars, and your employer has a satisfied employee and fewer payroll taxes to pay.

If you haven't already used an FSA, here's how it works. At the beginning of the year, you fill out a form telling your employer the amount of pretax money to be deducted from your paycheck and placed in your individual FSA. Read your plan carefully to understand the exact benefits available to you (more about this in the following subsections). Create a budget for expected expenses during the upcoming year and determine the amount you want your employer to set aside.

Then, as you pay for your benefits during the year, your employer periodically distributes the pretax dollars from the account to you. The FSA reimbursements show up as a nontaxable amount on your paycheck, or the plan may write you a separate check. Each employer has a detailed reimbursement procedure in place. Roadmap 7.1 shows what your actual tax savings could be from using $1,000 of FSA benefits.

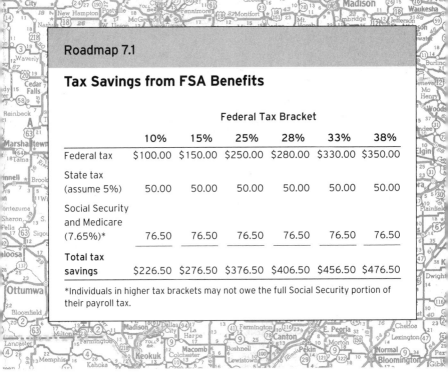

Roadmap 7.1

Tax Savings from FSA Benefits

	Federal Tax Bracket					
	10%	15%	25%	28%	33%	38%
Federal tax	$100.00	$150.00	$250.00	$280.00	$330.00	$350.00
State tax (assume 5%)	50.00	50.00	50.00	50.00	50.00	50.00
Social Security and Medicare (7.65%)*	76.50	76.50	76.50	76.50	76.50	76.50
Total tax savings	$226.50	$276.50	$376.50	$406.50	$456.50	$476.50

*Individuals in higher tax brackets may not owe the full Social Security portion of their payroll tax.

Another way the program sometimes works is that your employer specifies a certain bonus amount (let's say $1,000), and allows you either to put it into your FSA for reimbursement or to take the amount as cash. If it goes into the FSA, it works as described above and is tax-advantaged. If you take the cash, however, the entire amount is taxable.

There is, of course, a catch with an FSA: It's the old "use it or lose it." If you don't use the full amount of money you put aside in the FSA during a calendar year, you lose it at year's end. If this is your first year using the FSA strategy, you might want to be conservative with the amount you put in. Review the acceptable expenses and think carefully about how you might maximize your cash flow by using your FSA wisely. Let Uncle Sam subsidize the medicines (including over-the-counter medications), health care, child care, and other out-of-pocket costs that you will incur anyway. The tax savings can add up to real money in your checkbook.

As a rule, any health care expense you can deduct on your federal income tax is eligible for reimbursement from your Health Care FSA. In 2003, even over-the-counter remedies such as aspirin and cold medicine became acceptable for FSA reimbursement. So, if you are nearing year's end and have a hunch that you have not yet used all of your FSA withholdings, do a quick calculation and accelerate any qualified expenses that you can into the current tax year. If you do not use it, you lose it. Stocking up on bandages, antacids, and eye drops at tax-advantaged prices makes sense.

Dependent Care. Dependent care expenses at qualified day care centers for children (up to age 13) or disabled adults as well as home care costs are frequently eligible. To obtain the benefit, you must be paying for a dependent's day care so that you can work. In addition, if you are married, your spouse must work, attend school full-time at least five months each year, or be disabled.

Group Insurance. Group term life insurance (with some exceptions) is often available to employees as well as disability insurance.

Adoption Assistance. This benefit varies by employer plan.

Expenses Not Allowed. A cafeteria plan cannot reimburse you for the use of athletic facilities, educational assistance, meals, transportation, or employee discounts. Your benefits department can let you know what is and is not allowed.

▶ Long-Term Travel Plans: Managing Taxes on Your Investments

In addition to the tax deductions, credits, and breaks already described in this chapter, taxes are a critical element of successful investing. The benefit you gain from an investment is measured not only by how much you earn on it, but, ultimately, by how much of those earnings you keep. Therefore, although tax implications shouldn't drive your investment decisions, you should think about how you can minimize their impact on your investment earnings. Depending on your objectives, your income level, and whether you intend to itemize deductions, the ideas that follow can help you hold on to your earnings.

When you sell securities, you must pay taxes on any capital gains (which, in this case, includes the increase in a stock's value from the time that you first purchased the shares and any capital gain on which taxes have not been paid). The length of time you held the shares makes a big difference in the taxes owed. For example, if you sell an investment you held for 12 months or less, you pay your ordinary income tax rate on what is known as short-term capital gains. These rates are the same as your normal tax bracket. In contrast, if you held the investment for more than 12 months, you would qualify for the reduced capital gains rate.

Because you control when you sell a stock, the growth in the value of the stock is, in effect, a tax shelter. Particularly if the stock pays little or no dividend, all of the company's profits are reinvested in the business and, hopefully, make the stock's value rise over time. When you sell a stock you have held for at least 12 months, you pay a preferential capital gains tax rate. If you hold a stock bought after January 1, 2001, for at least five years, you will pay an 18 percent capital gains tax. This is a significantly lower tax than what you pay at regular income rates on dividend or interest income.

Be a Savvy Traveler: Contribute the Maximum to Tax-Advantaged Accounts

There are a variety of tax-advantaged accounts: retirement plans, education accounts, and tax-exempt securities. The following paragraphs explain each of them in more detail.

Retirement Plans. Plans like 401(k)s, 403(b)s, and traditional IRAs (as well as SEP-IRAs, SIMPLEs, and Keogh plans for the self-employed) offer multiple benefits for investors. Because the accounts are funded with pretax dollars, you pay lower taxes now (during the years that you contribute) and no taxes on the earnings until you start withdrawing funds. As an added bonus, some employers match a portion of your contributions to the retirement plan. It's essentially "free money," and you should take it!

Contributions to a Roth IRA, on the other hand, are made with after-tax money, but this money still grows tax free and can be withdrawn tax free when the account has been open more than five years and you are over age 59½. The advantages of Roth IRAs are numerous; aside from the retirement plan your employer may offer you, a Roth IRA may be the best wealth-building vehicle available. There are, however, some income limitations, and not everyone qualifies to open a Roth IRA. (Refer to Chapter 4 on retirement planning for more information on Roth IRAs.)

Education Accounts. Consider using 529 plans and education savings accounts to help save for education expenses. Withdrawals from these accounts are tax free if used for qualified higher education expenses. (Refer to Chapter 6 for more information.)

Tax-Exempt Securities. Consider how you can reduce taxes on investments in your taxable accounts. One way is to select tax-exempt securities, if they fit your investment objective. Such investments include the following:

State and local municipal bonds and bond funds. The interest on these funds is exempt from federal income taxes and state taxes in the state where the bond is issued, although state taxes may be due on municipal bonds issued by other states. Because interest is exempt, these bonds have a slightly higher effective yield than other taxable bonds, such as corporate bonds, particularly in states with higher state tax rates. These investments are typically best suited for investors in high tax brackets. To determine if your tax-exempt investment comes out ahead, compare the tax-equivalent yield of your investment to the yields of the taxable investments available.

For example, let's compare a municipal bond paying 2.2 percent (tax free) with an equivalent corporate bond yielding 3.0 percent. Converting the tax-free yield into a decimal, you get .0022. Divide that number by .75 (1.0 minus the tax rate of .25), you get a tax-equivalent yield of 2.93 percent. Therefore, if everything else is equal, the taxable bond at 3 percent will provide a slightly higher after-tax return than a tax-free bond. For this example, we did not take into account the state income tax. Here's the formula again.

Tax-equivalent yield = Tax-exempt yield ÷ (1 − your tax bracket)

U.S. Treasury securities. Interest on Treasury securities is exempt from state taxes, but not from federal income taxes. Investors who live in states with high income tax rates, but who are not necessarily in a high federal income tax bracket, may want to consider such investments to reduce their state income tax liability.

Series E and EE savings bonds. Unless you elect to report the interest annually, the interest on Series E and Series EE bonds is deferred until the year that you redeem the bond or until it reaches maturity.

If your modified AGI is above a certain level at the time you redeem your savings bonds (this amount is adjusted slightly upward for inflation every year), the interest you earn from the bonds is either fully or partially tax exempt if you use it for college tuition for either yourself, your spouse, or your children. This version of savings bonds is called an education bond, and it can apply to any bond purchased after December 31, 1989.

Try a Different Route: Invest in Tax-Efficient Securities in Taxable Accounts

Investors should consider the following alternatives for implementing a tax-efficient equity portfolio. Each option offers a degree of control over the timing of capital gains and losses when buying and selling individual stocks while facilitating diversification through mutual funds.

Exchange Traded Funds. ETFs are similar to index mutual funds but are traded on an exchange like a stock. They also are not redeemed, similar to a mutual fund. Thus, ETFs escape the capital gains that mutual funds face when selling stocks to redeem shares; but, like mutual funds, the annualized gains on ETFs must be recognized when the investment is sold.

Folios and Wrap Accounts. A folio is a basket of securities that investors prebuild or customize to their investment objectives. With folios, the investor (not a fund manager) executes trades, thereby controlling the timing of capital gains. With wrap accounts, the investor pays a financial professional to manage a portfolio that meets the investment objectives, which can include tax efficiency.

Traveling by Bus: Tax Strategies for Mutual Funds

You can also reduce your taxes on your mutual fund investments. Mutual funds must distribute their capital gains and dividend income to investors at least once per year. These distributions are subject to income taxes whether taken in cash or reinvested into the fund. Even in a down market, don't assume that your fund will not have capital gains to distribute. Capital gains result from stocks or bonds being sold at a profit, which means that even if your mutual fund posted a loss, you still could be hit with a capital gains distribution. Therefore, the following paragraphs offer some strategies to reduce the tax liability from your mutual fund investments.

Invest in Tax-Efficient Mutual Funds. Depending on how they are managed, some mutual funds generate a larger tax bill than others, so it pays to consider tax efficiency when choosing funds. To reduce tax liability, consider investing in a tax-managed fund or an index fund:

1. Tax-managed funds are those in which the fund manager takes steps to reduce capital gains distributions throughout the year by reducing the number of trades in the fund and by offsetting gains with losses before the end of the year.
2. Index funds are inherently tax efficient, because they are designed to track a benchmark (like the S&P 500). Benchmarks are baskets of selected stocks pooled together to represent the broad stock market or a specific segment of the market. Because the makeup of the baskets does not change regularly, the stocks aren't traded frequently, and the fund doesn't realize capital gains on the sale of appreciated stocks in the portfolio.

Invest in Tax-Exempt Municipal Bond Funds. Like individual state and local municipal bonds, the interest earned on municipal bond funds is exempt from both federal income taxes and state income taxes in the state in which the bonds originated. Thus, investors in high-income tax brackets reap the tax benefits of municipal bonds while also benefiting from the diversity, lower investment minimums, and professional management of mutual funds.

Time Your Investments Carefully. If you invest in a mutual fund late in the year, and that fund has realized significant capital gains during that year, you may be purchasing a tax liability. To avoid this pitfall, you should review funds for the estimated dates and amounts of capital gains distributions before you invest, and then purchase after the capital gains distributions have taken place. You can usually get information about expected capital gains distributions by calling the mutual fund company or visiting them online.

Harvest Tax Losses. Before the end of each year, make an inventory of the capital gains distributions that you have or expect to receive. If you have significant capital gains, consider selling an investment at a loss to offset some of those gains. You may even wish to consider this strategy in a down market when you do not have capital gains. This strategy is called harvesting tax losses. You may repurchase the same positions that you sold after 31 days, or you may purchase similar investments right away.

Identify Which Shares You Are Selling. Generally, if you sell shares of a fund in which you did not reinvest the dividends, all you need are the purchase and sale trade confirmations or the equivalent information. However, if you sold shares of a mutual fund in which you had the dividends and the capital gains reinvested, reporting the sale gets more involved.

The IRS allows you to determine which shares you are selling when you sell a portion of your stock or mutual fund holdings. The shares you specify will determine your tax liability. If you sell all the shares of a fund, your basis is the total cost of all purchases plus reinvested dividends and capital gains. If you sell only a portion of your shares, you can use one of four main methods to calculate the cost basis of mutual fund shares when reinvesting dividends:

1. *Average cost.* This method can be used if you purchased shares at various times and varying prices. But once you start using it, you can't switch to another method until the entire investment is liquidated. Generally this is the easiest way to calculate the cost basis. To compute your cost basis, simply add the total cost of all shares purchased (including reinvested dividends and capital gains), and then divide by the total number of shares you owned at the time of the sale. The result will be your average cost per share. Multiply the average cost per share by the number of shares sold, and subtract that number from the total sale proceeds. If the result is positive, you have a capital gain. In determining whether it is a long-term or short-term capital gain or loss, treat it as having sold your oldest shares first.

2. *Double category.* First, divide your shares into those held long-term (more than 12 months) and short-term (12 months or less). Then do a separate calculation for each category as above. This will give you the average cost basis of shares on a long-term and short-term basis; you report those separately on your tax return.

3. *First in, first out (FIFO).* The IRS assumes you are using the FIFO method. It is pretty simple when used with funds that do not reinvest dividends or capital gains distributions. However, it can be tough to calculate when reinvesting. The first shares purchased are considered to be the first shares sold.

4. *Specific Identification.* This method helps you determine your gain or loss by designating a specific purchase or lot of shares as the ones sold. You must notify your broker or discount brokerage firm of the specific shares

you are selling and get confirmation of that sale in writing, as proof of your actual intent to sell those specific shares. This method gives you the greatest control over matching the shares that you have sold; however, it is also the most time-consuming method, and good record keeping is a must.

Keep Good Records. To correctly identify which shares to sell requires good records. Each time you make a mutual fund purchase, keep track of the date of purchase, the number of shares that you buy, and the price that you paid for all original and subsequent shares purchased. Also keep track of all the shares that were reinvested (dividend and capital gains distributions should be automatically reinvested in most cases). These distributions are taxed in the year that they are received. If they are reinvested to buy more shares, these distributions should be added to the cost basis of your investment. This procedure will avoid double taxation when the shares are eventually sold.

You can save yourself and your accountant some trouble by setting up a spreadsheet of all your funds and individual stocks and their costs. Do this now to make tax time a little easier. At a minimum, retain copies of all the investment statements and trade confirmations on your personally held securities.

If you and your spouse own individual stocks, keep records of stock splits, spin-offs, and mergers so that later you have the historical information to accurately assess the implications of the capital gains and losses. You might find that using a software program, such as Quicken or MS Money, and by using the financial Web sites of your brokerage firm and Yahoo, for example, are easy ways to keep track of this information.

▶ Don't Make a Wrong Turn: Avoid Mistakes in Tax Deductions

The earlier you and your spouse begin your tax strategy, the more successful you will be in achieving your objectives and maximizing your deductions. Here are a few common mistakes that you can easily avoid when filing your income taxes.

Think Smart When Claiming Dependents. As mentioned earlier in the chapter, if you can claim a parent, grandparent, nephew, niece, brother, or sister as a dependent on your tax return, you probably can file as head of household. Remember that if you have just had a baby, you need to get a Social Security number for the child before filing your tax return. The IRS will not allow you to claim a dependency exemption, child tax credit, or earned income credit without a valid Social Security number.

If you have children from your previous marriage, and your ex-spouse claims your child as a dependent on his or her tax return, but the child lives with you, then you probably still can file as head of household. A custodial parent who has given an ex-spouse the right to claim a child as a dependent still has the right to claim head of household status, the earned income credit, and dependent care credit. However, whoever claims the dependency exemption also should claim the child tax credit.

Remember that Charitable Contributions Are Tax Deductible. The last section of the chapter describes how to donate from your investing portfolio to charity, but don't overlook other ways to donate and deduct. Millions of Americans fail to claim the full value of their charitable donations each year. If you donate old clothes, furniture, appliances, and other items to a favorite charity, claim the charitable contribution deduction for the fair market value of the donated items. These deductions mount up. Be sure that you get a written receipt from the charity for donations of $250 or more; this rule applies whether you are donating cash (or paying by check) or goods.

H&R Block (http://www.hrblock.com) offers DeductionPro, a software application, to help folks determine the value of their charitable donations. The $20 program helps put fair market values on the most commonly donated household items, including clothing, baby accessories, linens, furniture, household appliances, and more. Another software program, It's Deductible: Turning Donations into Dollars (http://www.itsdeductible.com) from Intuit costs $20 and includes guidance in tracking other miscellaneous expenses.

Make Your Deductions in One Year. To get the most benefit from your deductions on your income tax return, organize them so that they all occur during one year to ensure that you exceed the minimum requirements. Keep in mind, however, that you can deduct only those medical expenses in excess of 7.5 percent of your adjusted gross income, and only those miscellaneous itemized deductions in excess of 2 percent of your AGI.

To be successful in grouping your deductions, your plans must be developed long before tax-filing day arrives. As the end of the year nears, check your eligibility for various deductions. Then look for other expenses that can be arranged to send you over the threshold for each deduction you are eligible for.

Keep Good Records! Don't exaggerate expenses to rack up deductions. If you're ever audited, you will need to be able to prove that your deductions are valid. Be sure your tax return line items match the 1099s you receive from your broker, employer, and investment company. The IRS receives a copy of all 1099s, so they can match what's on your tax return with what's on the 1099s. Avoid discrepancies. Here are some useful Web sites:

1. The IRS Web site (http://www.irs.gov) offers valuable tax information on everything from answers to commonly asked questions to tax tips. It also tells you how to e-file, how to get copies of forms, and much more.
2. Bankrate.com (http://www.bankrate.com) offers a wealth of free tax and other financial information.

Keep a Travel Log: Make Sure You and Your Spouse Have Good Records

Keeping good records has been mentioned quite a few times in this chapter —and for good reason. With two people's finances at stake, you want to be sure that your situation and your future are secure. Many couples worry about turning over all the finances to one partner, yet as described in Chapter 1, it's the best way for a couple to maintain control of their money. Once again, keep in mind that it doesn't always have to be the same person who's the "family budget director." There's no reason why you can't trade off from time to time.

Still, there are a few things you should consider to stay in the good graces of the IRS. First of all, get organized so you don't have to worry about being audited. If you do receive an IRS notice that says you owe additional tax, most likely it's the result of an IRS error, not yours. Many times, these issues can be resolved with a phone call. Check out the facts first; don't blindly pay the amount requested. You can avoid or at least reduce the trauma of an IRS audit by being prepared. The most efficient way to do that is when your tax return is prepared, not three years later when you suddenly receive a notice in the mail requesting information from the past. For some suggestions on how to get and stay organized, see "What to Pack" on the following page.

What to Pack

Financial Records You Need in Case You Get Audited

▶ Keep records of payments (ledgers, receipts, check copies, invoices) and all other pertinent documents with your tax returns.

▶ Organize your receipts for charitable contributions, both cash and noncash. Contributions in amounts of $250 or more at any one time require written acknowledgment from the charitable entity stating that you received no tangible benefit for your contribution. These statements need to be dated and in your possession at the time you file your return to make your contribution deductible.

▶ Noncash contributions, such as appreciated stock or personal goods, require signed receipts from the charitable entity. If the amounts are more than $500, you must complete IRS Form 8283, showing the date of your contribution, the entity to which you donated, the entity's address, the date you acquired the item, the cost of the item, the fair market value you're claiming, and the method you used to determine fair market value. (Not filing this form or filling it out improperly could prompt an inquiry.)

▶ If you're selling property, make sure that you have credible documentation that supports the cost you're claiming for that property. This can be difficult to obtain when gifts received from relatives long ago are involved. (If you give property as a gift, include the documentation for the recipient's files.) If you must file a gift tax return, the information will be on that return, so just give the individual a copy of the return.

Pack Your Bags: How Long to Keep Certain Records

Being prepared also means keeping records for an adequate length of time. Here's an easy guideline:

1. Store the following records permanently: tax returns, financial statements, corporate stock, corporate records and minutes, and real estate records.

2. Keep the following records to support your tax returns for at least the length of time that you could possibly be audited, which is usually seven years: bank statements and canceled checks that are pertinent to the tax return, mileage, travel and entertainment records, other receipts, and acknowledgments.

3. Keep the following property-related records for as long as you own the property plus seven years: asset and depreciation records, home purchase and improvement records, and investment records.

Make Sure Your Map Is Accurate: Ensuring a Correct Tax Return

A simple though sometimes time-consuming way to gain peace of mind with your income tax filings is to check your information and your return carefully before mailing it. Here's a starting list.

1. Be sure that names and Social Security numbers on the return match the numbers on each individual's Social Security card. (This is particularly important for newly married individuals.)
2. Record the correct Social Security numbers or identification numbers for child care providers.
3. If one of you pays or receives alimony, make sure the alimony that is deducted for one ex-spouse is the same amount as the alimony reported for the other ex-spouse.
4. Check that your estimated payments are entered in the correct amounts.
5. Make sure all items are entered on the correct lines, and double check your math!

If You Get Pulled Over: What to Do If You're Audited

No doubt about it, an IRS audit is a hassle. But if you're prepared and approach the audit in a professional manner, it most likely will be resolved satisfactorily. Here is the recommended approach.

1. Respond promptly to the notice as requested.
2. Plan to approach the audit with a professional at your side or arrange to have someone represent you.
3. Gather all the documentation you organized and placed with the copy of your tax return when it was filed.
4. Pull only the documents requested and no more.
5. Remember that IRS agents are people with homes and family, just like you. Be courteous and treat them as you would like to be treated.
6. Respond to direct questions but volunteer no additional information.
7. Do not sign anything without reviewing it carefully. Get the opinion of a tax professional as to the ramifications of any document you are asked to sign.

Additional information about keeping good records and avoiding audits is available at http://www.finance.cch.com/text/c60s05d070.asp. The information, calculators, and resources there are provided by CCH Incorporated (http://www.finance.cch.com) and Meara King (http://www.mearaking.com).

If Your Car Breaks Down: What to Do if One Spouse Hasn't Filed a Tax Return

If, during your financial discussions with your future spouse, you find that he or she hasn't filed a tax return for one or more years, don't despair. (Or perhaps you are the one to confess to this misdeed.) Failure to file is often due to a traumatic event in someone's life, such as loss of employment, divorce, or family sickness, events that can be devastating all by themselves. Failure to file also occurs after a sudden increase in income, which results in an unexpected, large amount of taxes due. When people can't pay the taxes, they sometimes become so disconcerted that they don't file a tax return. When a tax year is missed and nothing bad happens, they sometimes skip the next year. The illusion that nothing will happen creates a false sense of security.

The first indication that the IRS has that you or your spouse has not filed a return is often a levy on your wages. This event might, in fact, be your first wake-up call as well. You may have moved and forgot to send a change of address to the IRS. (The IRS, by law, sends its notices to the taxpayer's last known address.) To complicate matters, after six months, the post office will no longer forward your mail, so you are unaware that the IRS is trying to reach you. However, the IRS has a current W-2 or 1099 form provided by your employer or customer. The IRS may use that information to garnish (or directly deduct money from) your wages.

If you own a business with a sizable amount of cash transactions and have not been filing tax returns, the IRS may already have accumulated a large amount of information on you. For instance, they may be aware of real estate, cars, trucks, boats, airplanes, RVs, bank accounts, and cash transactions reported to the IRS as well as 1098 interest paid on residential housing. They may also know where you live, the name of your spouse's employer, or any of your transfers of assets.

If you need to be convinced further about why it's important to file your tax returns promptly, here are four more reasons:

1. Interest and penalties will accrue from the due date on the amount of tax due.
2. After three years of not filing returns, even if you have a refund due, the IRS will not pay it to you.
3. You will lose any earned income credits or child tax credits.
4. The statute of limitations on collections of monies due will not start until a tax return is filed and the tax assessed. Many times, the IRS will file a return for the taxpayer called an SFR (a service filed return). This SFR is filed according to the category "taxpayer single" with no itemized deductions, which results in the highest tax possible being assessed. The statute also does not run on an SFR return.

Of course, being convinced of the reasons to file doesn't help you if you've already failed to file. So let's focus on the road ahead, instead of what's in the rearview mirror. Here's what you should do now:

1. *Consult a qualified tax attorney.* This consultation is especially important if there is any reason to believe that the IRS might consider that your nonfiling was willful. Such an action could be considered fraud. A tax attorney has attorney-client privilege, and any information you and your spouse share with him or her cannot be revealed to the IRS, provided that the attorney does not prepare your delinquent tax returns. Your attorney can then hire a qualified tax preparer to prepare your delinquent returns.
2. *Get your past tax returns prepared.* If you do not have any of your W-2s or 1099s, you can get this information from the IRS. If you file voluntarily before the IRS contacts you, submit returns for the last six years. Otherwise, file all the years that the IRS requests. Be sure that the returns are accurate and all income is reported. There is no statute of limitations on a fraudulent return, and even an amended fraudulent return is still considered fraudulent.
3. *If the IRS decides to examine your delinquent returns, do not attend the examination.* Hire an Enrolled Agent, a CPA, or an attorney who practices representation of taxpayers before the IRS. If the IRS summons you to appear, you must appear, but you do not have to testify. The IRS might intimidate you if you go to an examination alone, which could be serious and injurious to your tax situation.

4. *Always request an abatement of any penalties if there is reasonable cause.*
A reasonable cause could include continued unemployment, divorce,
drug addiction, or serious medical problems.

After your delinquent tax returns have been processed and the tax assessed, there are only four ways to settle a collection issue:

1. Pay the tax in full.
2. Enter into an installment payment agreement.
3. Get the taxes owed classified as currently uncollectible.
4. Do an "offer in compromise" and settle the tax debt for less than full
value.

Finally, keep in mind for the future that it's better for you and your
spouse to stay current on filing your tax returns, even if you cannot pay
your taxes all at once.

Appendix A

An Itinerary

Here's a quick review of what to do as you set out on the financial road to getting married:

1. Talk candidly about your finances (his, hers, and ours) and make a plan for how you want to spend, save, and invest for your financial future together.

   ▶ Discuss how to handle your savings and checking accounts and your taxes.
   ▶ Get organized: Set up a financial filing system, and decide which of you will manage the money and pay the bills.
   ▶ Establish an emergency fund, in case one of you becomes ill, has an accident, or stops working.
   ▶ Create a budget you both can live with: Find out what you're each currently spending money on, and decide if that's how you want to spend it.
   ▶ Discuss your short-term and long-term financial goals. Are you saving for retirement, buying a second home, or educating your children and grandchildren?

2. If you decide to buy a home, calculate what you can afford and decide which type of mortgage is best for you.

   ▶ Get preapproval for a mortgage so you don't waste time looking at homes you can't afford.
   ▶ Find out how your credit record looks and learn ways to improve it if you need to.
   ▶ Calculate how much house you can afford, what your mortgage tax deduction would be, and what your tax savings would be if you buy a house.
   ▶ Decide which of five types of mortgages best fits your specific financial situation.

> ▶ Consider whether you want to buy a traditional house or a condo, co-op, or townhouse.

3. Get the right insurance to protect yourself, your spouse, and your family if you plan to have children.

> ▶ Calculate how much and what type of life insurance coverage you need so you won't waste your money on unnecessary coverage.
> ▶ Get enough disability insurance to protect you if you have an accident or become ill and can't work, so that you and your spouse can still pay your bills.
> ▶ Choose the right health insurance plan for your medical needs: HMO, PPO, or a traditional fee-for-service plan.
> ▶ Find out how much homeowners insurance you need to protect your home (and your possessions) from fire, theft, earthquakes, and floods.
> ▶ Learn what to expect in terms of changing your insurance if and when you have children.
> ▶ Integrate your insurance plans with your estate planning, to maximize your long-term investments.

4. Start planning now for your retirement so you can retire comfortably when you want to.

> ▶ Decide how you and your spouse want to spend your retirement, and determine what that might cost. Project your expenses and income during your retirement years so you can start saving and investing now.
> ▶ Calculate how much you'll need to save for retirement and where that money will come from: Social Security benefits, your 401(k)s or other employer pension plans, and your own savings and investments.
> ▶ Determine your risk tolerance for different types of investments.
> ▶ Find out how you can maximize your investments now to ease your future financial situation.

5. Make your wills and an estate plan to ensure your heirs will be protected financially after you're gone.

> ▶ Find out what estate planning entails, and what can happen to your assets if you don't have one: It isn't pretty!

- ▶ Learn how your estate may be taxed so you can reduce the so-called death tax.
- ▶ If you've been married before or already have children, discover what you need to know to protect all your heirs.
- ▶ Make sure that both you and your spouse prepare separate wills. Find out what other documents you should have, such as a living will, a power of attorney for financial decisions, and a power of attorney for health care decisions.
- ▶ Discover ways to reduce probate so more of your assets can be passed on to whom you want, rather than the IRS.
- ▶ Know how marital property laws affect how you can bequeath your assets.

6. If you're planning to have children, save and invest for their educations so you're not knocked out financially in 20 years:

- ▶ Calculate how much you'll need to save.
- ▶ Try saving $100 each month to see how money can accumulate.
- ▶ Learn about the various ways to save and invest for college: 529 plans, prepaid tuition plans, bonds, custodial accounts, Coverdell savings accounts, and other plans. Find the ones that are best for your situation.
- ▶ Choose the right investment vehicle for your needs: individual stocks, different types of bonds, mutual funds, to name a few.
- ▶ Find out how various forms of financial aid can help you when your kids are approaching their college years.

7. Know how your tax situation will change once you're married:

- ▶ Find out how your tax rates and tax brackets will be different with two incomes.
- ▶ Discover the deductions that you can legally take on your tax return, especially those relating to your mortgage and property taxes if you own your home.
- ▶ Know which tax credits can reduce your taxes, including those concerning children (born or adopted), education, business, and others.

- ▶ Find out more about how careful estate planning can improve your tax situation, including putting money in trusts and giving away your assets during your lifetime.
- ▶ Get tax breaks from employee benefits, such as flexible spending accounts.
- ▶ Manage your investments to minimize your taxes.
- ▶ Make sure you and your spouse keep good records to avoid problems, additional taxes, or audits.

Bon voyage on your new life together!

Appendix B

The Best of *Getting Married*: A Resource Guide

▶ Bibliography

The following books were used as resources for this book. In addition, we have provided lists of other books and Web sites that offer more detailed information on some of the topics covered. We hope you find all of these resources useful.

Barney, Colleen and Victoria Collins. *Best Intentions: Ensuring Your Estate Plan Delivers both Wealth and Wisdom.* Chicago: Dearborn Trade Publishing, 2002.

Cook, Frank. *You're Not Buying That House, Are You? Everything You May Forget to Do, Ask, or Think about before Signing on the Dotted Line.* Chicago: Dearborn Trade Publishing, 2004.

Garrett, Sheryl. *Just Give Me the Answers: Expert Advisors Address Your Most Pressing Financial Questions.* Chicago: Dearborn Trade Publishing, 2004.

Garton-Good, Julie. *All about Mortgages: Insider Tips to Finance or Refinance Your Home,* 3rd ed. Chicago: Dearborn Trade Publishing, 2004.

Goodman, Jordan E. *Everyone's Money Book,* 3rd ed. Chicago: Dearborn Trade Publishing, 2001.

Irwin, Robert. *Buy Your First Home!* 2nd ed. Chicago: Dearborn Trade Publishing, 2000.

Lank, Edith. *The HomeBuyer's Kit,* 5th ed. With Dena Amoruso. Chicago: Dearborn Trade Publishing, 2001.

Lewis, Allyson. *The Million Dollar Car and $250,000 Pizza: How Every Dollar You Save Builds Your Financial Future.* Chicago: Dearborn Trade Publishing, 2000.

Magee, David S. and John Ventura. *Everything Your Heirs Need to Know,* 3rd ed, Chicago: Dearborn Trade Publishing, 1999.

McNaughton, Deborah. *All about Credit: Questions (and Answers) about the Most Common Credit Problems.* Chicago: Dearborn Trade Publishing, 1999.

Steinmetz, Thomas C. *The Mortgage Kit,* 5th ed. Chicago: Dearborn Trade Publishing, 2002.

Ventura, John. *The Will Kit.* 2nd ed. Chicago: Dearborn Trade Publishing, 2002.

Weiss, Mark. *Condos, Co-Ops, and Townhomes: A Complete Guide to Finding, Buying, Maintaining, and Enjoying Your New Home.* Chicago: Dearborn Trade Publishing, 2003.

▶ Recommended Books and Web Sites

Chapter 2: A New Destination: Buying a Home Together

Irwin, Robert. *Buying a Home on the Internet.* New York: McGraw-Hill, 1999.

_____. *Tips and Traps When Mortgage Hunting.* 2nd ed. New York: McGraw-Hill, 1998.

Chapter 3: The Ultimate Air Bag: Insurance to Protect Your Spouse and Family

Best Web Sites for Insurance Information

Here are some of the best insurance information sites for solid educational content, policy quotes, or links to quote services. Doing your homework ahead of time can save you money on premiums—and headaches down the road.

- ▶ About Disability Insurance (http://www.about-disability-insurance.com) provides descriptions of the major features of a disability insurance policy and links to other Web sites.
- ▶ E.F. Moody (http://www.efmoody.com), a life and disability insurance analyst, features financial information as well as an overview of insurance.
- ▶ Federal Emergency Management Agency (FEMA) flood insurance information (http://www.fema.gov/nfip/whonfip.shtm) offers the only option

for flood coverage. This site provides information about the coverage and how to get it.

▶ Health Insurance Information (http://www.healthinsuranceinfo.net) is a resource that provides information on how to maintain health insurance once COBRA coverage expires. See the "Consumer Guides for Getting and Keeping Insurance" for each state.

▶ Insurance Information Institute (http://www.iii.org) provides the public with information about insurance and the insurance industry.

▶ Insure Kids Now (www.insurekidsnow.gov) offers information on free or low-cost health insurance to children of lower-income families who do not have health insurance.

▶ Medicare (http://www.hhs.gov) includes Medigap plan comparisons, Medicare health plans comparisons, and consumer publications as well as directories of potential sources of additional assistance for managing health care expenses.

▶ National Association of Insurance Commissioners (http://www.naic. org) is a consumer interest site featuring a directory of state insurance regulators and a catalog of educational publications.

Insurance Rating Agencies and Helpful Sites

▶ A.M. Best Company (http://www.ambest.com)

▶ Anthony Steuer Insurance Services (http://www.tonysteuer.com/res_RatingServices.html)

▶ Coalition against Insurance Fraud—Scam Alerts and Insurance Fraud Hall of Shame (http://www.insurancefraud.org)

▶ Fitch Ratings, Ltd. (http://www.fitchratings.com)

▶ Moody's Investor Services (http://www.moodys.com)

▶ Standard and Poor's Corporation (http://www.standardandpoors.com)

▶ Weiss Research (http://www.weissratings.com)

Insurance Shopping Sites to Compare and Obtain Quotes

▶ http://www.insweb.com

▶ http://www.insure.com

▶ http://www.ehealthinsurance.com

▶ http://moneycentral.msn.com/insure/welcome.asp

Chapter 5: The End of the Journey: Estate Planning and Making a Will
Finding a Financial Planner

▶ Garrett Planning Network (http://www.GarrettPlanningNetwork.com) is the nation's premier organization of hourly, fee-only financial planners. The site offers information on how financial planners differ. Enter through the "Consumers" button, which includes a "Locate an Advisor" link.

▶ The National Association of Personal Financial Planners (http://www.napfa.org) offers a questionnaire that you can use to interview potential financial planners. Check out the "Consumer Tips" link; which includes a "Find a Napfa Registered Financial Advisor" link.

▶ Certified Financial Planners Board of Standards (http://www.cfp-board.org) is the organization that awards the CFP® marks of distinction. This site offers insights on how financial planners are credentialed.

▶ The Financial Planning Association (http://www.fpanet.org) site offers a questionnaire that you can use to interview potential financial planners. Click on the "Public" button, then locate the "Searching for a Financial Planner?" link.

Chapter 6: Traveling with Children: Saving for Your Kids' College Education

There are many books, Web sites, and other resources available on how to find college scholarships, parent and student loans, and grant money for your children's college educations, but because you won't really need to consult them for at least another 15–20 years, the following information focuses on resources that can help you now, when you're just beginning to deal with the financial concerns and considerations you need to make as a married couple.

Books

▶ *Paying for Your Child's College Education* by Marguerite Smith. Time Warner, 3 Center Plaza, Boston, MA 02108. Telephone: 1-800-343-9204 (http://www.timewarner.com). From *Money* magazine, offers precise short-and long-term plans, helpful graphs, and worksheets to help parents set aside money for school, whether the child is 18 years or 18 months old.

Software

▶ Financial Aid (EFC) (Octameron Associates, P.O. Box 2748, Alexandria, VA 22301. Telephone: 1-703-836-3480 (http://www.octameron.com). A simple software program designed to help you compute your expected family contribution to college costs. By changing the income or assets that your family reports, you can easily see how your expected contribution changes. This program may also help you find ways to lower your expected family contribution and, thus, qualify for more student aid.

State-Sponsored College Savings Programs

Many states offer plans in which residents can save money for college expenses and also get a tax break. The money in the account accumulates tax deferred. Even though the assets are held in the name of the parents, they are taxed at the child's lower tax rate when they start college. Most state programs keep the money in conservative investments, such as Treasury securities, and therefore pay a relatively low rate of return. Other states, such as Indiana, invest the money in a mix of stocks and bonds, offering participants higher potential rates of return, but with more risk. Check with your state to see how the money is invested.

▶ Alaska College Savings Program: 1-907-474-5927

▶ Arizona Family College Savings Program: 1-602-229-2591

▶ Arkansas GIFT College Investing Plan: 1-877-422-6553

▶ California Golden State ScholarShare Trust: 1-877-728-4338

▶ Colorado Scholars Choice College Savings Program: 1-800-478-5651

▶ Connecticut Higher Education Trust: 1-888-799-2438

▶ Delaware College Investment Plan: 1-800-292-7935

▶ Florida College Savings Program: 1-800-552-4723

▶ Georgia HOPE Scholarship: 1-800-776-6878

▶ Hawaii College Savings Program: 1-808-586-1518

▶ Idaho College Savings Plan: 1-208-334-3200

▶ Illinois College Savings Pool: 1-217-782-1319

▶ Indiana Family College Savings Program: 1-888-814-6800

▶ Iowa College Savings: 1-888-672-9116

▶ Kansas Postsecondary Education Plan: 1-785-296-3171

▶ Kentucky Educational Savings Plan Trust: 1-877-598-7878

▶ Louisiana START: 1-800-259-5626, × 0523

- ► Maine NexGen College Investing Plan: 1-877-668-1116
- ► Maryland College Savings Plan: 1-888-463-4723
- ► Massachusetts U. Fund: 1-800-449-6332
- ► Michigan Education Savings Program: 1-800-638-4543
- ► Minnesota EDVEST: 1-800-657-3866, x3201
- ► Mississippi Affordable College Savings: 1-601-359-3600
- ► Missouri Family Higher Education Savings Plan: 1-888-414-6678
- ► Montana Family Education Savings Program: 1-800-888-2723
- ► Nebraska College Savings Plan: 1-402-471-3130
- ► New Hampshire Unique College Investing Plan: 1-800-544-1722
- ► New Jersey Better Educational Savings Trust: 1-877-465-2378
- ► New York's College Savings Program: 1-877-697-2837
- ► North Carolina College Vision Fund: 1-800-600-3453
- ► North Dakota College SAVE: 1-800-472-2166
- ► Ohio College Savings Program: 1-800-233-6734
- ► Oklahoma College Savings Plan: 1-405-858-4422
- ► Oregon Qualified Tuition Savings Program: 1-503-378-4329
- ► Pennsylvania Investment Savings Program: 1-800-440-4000
- ► Rhode Island Higher Education Savings Trust: 1-877-474-4378
- ► Tennessee Investment Savings Program: 1-888-486-2378
- ► Utah Educational Savings Plan Trust: 1-800-418-2551
- ► Vermont Higher Education Savings Plan: 1-800-637-5860
- ► Virginia Savings Plan Trust: 1-888-567-0540
- ► West Virginia Investors Program: 1-800-307-4701
- ► Wisconsin EDVEST: 1-888-338-3789
- ► Wyoming Family College Savings Program: 1-307-777-7408

Web Sites

- ► College Parents of America (http://www.collegeparents.org) requires membership, which costs $25. It provides information on saving strategies, financial aid, education tax credits and deductions, and other ways to help pay for college. It also offers members special values and discounts on items, such as computers, books, college guides, and study abroad programs.
- ► College Savings Plans Network (http://www.collegesavings.org) is designed to administer college savings plans. College savings plans allow participants to save money in a special college savings account on behalf

of a designated beneficiary's qualified higher education expenses. Contributions can vary, depending on the individual's savings goals. The plans offer a variable rate of return, although some programs guarantee a minimum rate of return. The College Savings Plans Network is an affiliate of the National Association of State Treasurers.

▶ Fidelity (http://www.fidelity.com). Click on "College Planning" and you will find a concise explanation of Section 529 college savings plans, along with comparisons of those plans with other prepaid tuition plans, such as Coverdell Savings Plans, taxable brokerage accounts, and Education IRAs.

▶ Saving for College.com (http://www.savingforcollege.com) includes a lot of information about college funding and provides access to a college savings calculator and a nationwide college tuition database. It provides information about Section 529 college savings plans and includes details of all the state government college financing plans. Just select your state and the information appears. Click on the "College Planning Resources" section to access this information. This Web site is considered by many to be the best on the subject of college funding.

▶ TIAA-CREF (http://www.tiaa-cref.org/) serves as investment manager for state-sponsored college savings programs, Education IRAs, prepaid tuition plans, and other college loans. TIAA-CREF charges an annual fee of .8% of account assets for its services.

Chapter 7: Paying Tolls: Handling Taxes as a Married Couple

Czaplyski, Lawrence and Vincent. *The Homeowner's Property Tax Relief Kit.* New York: McGraw-Hill, 1993.

Irwin, Robert. *The Landlord's Troubleshooter.* Chicago: Dearborn Trade Publishing, 1999.

Index

Notes

Notes

Get *On the Road* with Kaplan Publishing's Personal Finance Series

Starting **Out**

Buying a **Home**

Getting **Married**

Surviving the **Loss of a Spouse**

Planning an **Estate**

Saving/Paying for **College**

Surviving **Divorce**

Caring for an **Aging Parent**

The *On the Road* series is available at neighborhood and online booksellers. The series provides cradle to grave advice on personal finance issues.

Share the message!

Bulk discounts
Discounts start at only 10 copies and range from 30% to 55% off retail price based on quantity.

Custom publishing
Private label a cover with your organization's name and logo. Or, tailor information to your needs with a custom pamphlet that highlights specific chapters.

Ancillaries
Workshop outlines, videos, and other products are available on select titles.

Dynamic speakers
Engaging authors are available to share their expertise and insight at your event.

Call Dearborn Trade Special Sales at 1-800-621-9621, ext. 4444, or e-mail trade@dearborn.com.

Dearborn™
Trade Publishing
A **Kaplan Professional** Company